SACRAMENTO PUBLIC LIBRARY

D0758670

Cl

828 I STREET
SACRAMENTO, CA 95814
SEP - 1999

AMERICAN
YOUTH
VIOLENCE

AMERICAN

YOUTH

VIOLENCE

Franklin E. Zimring

New York   Oxford

Oxford University Press

1998

A MacArthur Juvenile Justice Network Study

Oxford University Press

Oxford   New York
Athens   Auckland   Bangkok   Bogotá Buenos Aires   Calcutta
Cape Town   Chennai   Dar es Salaam   Delhi   Florence   Hong Kong   Istanbul
Karachi   Kuala Lumpur   Madrid   Melbourne   Mexico City   Mumbai
Nairobi   Paris   São Paulo   Singapore   Taipei   Tokyo   Toronto   Warsaw

and associated companies in
Berlin   Ibadan

Copyright © 1998 by Oxford University Press, Inc.

Published by Oxford University Press, Inc.
198 Madison Avenue, New York, New York 10016

Oxford is a registered trademark of Oxford University Press

All rights reserved. No part of this publication may be reproduced,
stored in a retrieval system, or transmitted, in any form or by any means,
electronic, mechanical, photocopying, recording, or otherwise,
without the prior permission of Oxford University Press.

Library of Congress Cataloging-in-Publication Data
Zimring, Franklin E.
American youth violence / Franklin E. Zimring.
p.   cm.—(Studies in crime and public policy)
Includes bibliographical references and index.
ISBN 0-19-512145-7
1. Juvenile delinquency—Government policy—United States.
2. Violent crimes—Government policy—United States. 3. Juvenile
justice, Administration of—United States.   I. Title.   II. Series.
HV9104.Z57   1998
364.36′0973—dc21   98-3330

9 8 7 6 5 4 3 2

Printed in the United States of America
on acid-free paper

For Frank Allen and Gordon Hawkins

Acknowledgments

The study that produced this volume was commissioned and supported by the John D. and Catherine T. MacArthur Foundation in Chicago. Laurie Garduque of the MacArthur Foundation provided important substantive and administrative guidance during the study and the preparation of the book.

The research help of many people informs this book. June Kim, Sam Kamin, and William Nelson provided general assistance. Emily Chow did the study of media coverage in 1975 and in the 1990s that is reported in chapter 1. Marquette Jones researched federal gun legislation. Isabel Traugott did legislative, appellate case, and statistical research on transfers from juvenile to criminal court and on blended jurisdiction. James C. Howell read and improved early drafts of chapters 7 and 9. Philip J. Cook provided a methodological tutorial in the analysis of the case fatality rate in chapter 3, as well as comments on chapter 6.

Lee Robins and Francis Allen served as advisors on the project throughout 1997. They reviewed draft chapters and participated in a review of the manuscript in Chicago in December 1997. This process was immensely helpful. If an all-day meeting in the company of Robins and Allen does not produce symptoms of humility in an aspiring author, then nothing will.

Several colleagues read and criticized large portions of the manuscript, including Jeffrey Fagan, Tom Grisso, Robert Schwartz, Elizabeth Scott, and Larry Steinberg of the MacArthur Foundation Network on Adolescent Development and Juvenile Justice. Kevin Reitz of the University of Colorado and Barry Feld of the University of Minnesota reviewed the entire manuscript. Indeed, Professor Reitz read one more chapter than anyone else will ever be subjected to (as a result of his editorial advice). Michael Tonry and Mark Moore read and criticized a version of chapter 5 that appears in Volume 24 of *Crime and Justice: An Annual Review of Research.* Howard Snyder and Melissa Sickmund of the National Center on Juvenile Justice read and commented on chapters 1 to 4.

The help I received from Gordon Hawkins is an embarrassment to report. Over the summer of 1997, he was an active collaborator in drafting chapters 6, 7, and 9. Those who wonder whether Zimring can write without Hawkins will not get a good answer from the contents of this volume.

The Earl Warren Legal Institute at the University of California at Berkeley is a terrific place to write books, in large part because of the skill and good humor of Karen Chin, our administrative guru. Toni Mendicino produced countless drafts of each chapter in this volume without any visible deficit in patience and good humor.

Contents

Introduction

This book is about violent acts by adolescent offenders and the legal principles and institutions that respond to youth violence. The focus of this study is narrow in two important respects. First, the violent acts discussed here are only those committed by offenders under the age of 18, less than a quarter of all life-threatening violence in the United States. If serious violence is the subject of concern, devoting a sustained analysis only to offenders under 18 misses more than three-quarters of the problem. The second major limit of the study is that only one type of adolescent deviance is under scrutiny. More than 80 percent of all juvenile law violations are not violent. If juvenile crime is the topic of concern, a book-length study of only those acts that inflict or threaten bodily harm will ignore the great majority of youth crimes.

Yet adolescent violence has been throughout the 1990s a special focus of concern in American society and government. Commentators and legislators worry about adolescent violence (and not the violence of older offenders) because it is believed that youth violence, alone, is increasing and is likely to continue increasing. Adolescent violence is considered a separate problem from other forms of youth crime because of the larger harm that violent acts cause and because serious violence by young offenders in the 1990s is believed to be an indication that American cities are witnessing the emergence of a more dangerous breed of juvenile offender, whose vicious behavior is unprecedented and whose numbers can only grow in the first decade of the next century.

In the first seven years of the 1990s, virtually every state in the United States has changed the laws designed to cope with violence by offenders under 18, and the U.S. Congress and executive branch have been debating far-reaching proposals about juvenile and criminal justice to respond to levels of youth violence that are regarded as a national emergency.

This book aims to be a relatively comprehensive examination of youth violence in the United States. The study is reported in three installments. Part I is an empirical examination of youth violence in the 1990s. Chapter 1 describes the crisis mood surrounding youth violence in the 1990s and compares the media coverage and legislative responses of recent years to earlier periods of special focus on juvenile crime. Chapter 2 explores the special character of adolescent violence in the United States, comparing patterns and rates of violent crimes by adolescents with typical violence by older offenders. Chapters 3 and 4 directly address the factual evidence of crisis conditions. Chapter 3 examines the evidence on trends in serious youth violence since 1980. Chapter 4 analizes population trends and projections over the period 1960 to 2010, responding to fears that a "boomerang" rebound in the youth population will create substantial increases in the volume of serious violence.

The second part of this study examines the legal principles and specific policy options available to respond to violent acts by early and middle adolescents. Chapter 5 sets out basic principles that should inform policy choices. Chapter 6 is a review of strategies and tactics to control the risks of the adolescent misuse of guns. Because the increase in fatalities attributable to young offenders was almost exclusively an increase in gun cases, firearms policy is an unavoidable topic in a balanced review of youth violence. Chapter 7 discusses standards for transfer of juveniles accused of violent crime to criminal courts. Such standards are the usual legislative response to public concerns about youth violence. Chapter 8 discusses the legal system's responses to adolescents who kill. Homicide cases produce by far the most serious harm from youth violence. They are also the most difficult cases for finding a balance between mitigation and penal harshness in legal policy. Coherent principles for homicides are the ultimate challenge for a youth violence policy.

The last section attempts to put the debate about youth violence into two broader contexts. Chapter 9 discusses youth violence and the future of the juvenile court. Do violence cases belong in the juvenile court? Should powers of punishment be expanded when adolescents do great bodily harm? Chapter 10 concludes the study with an examination of the current concern about youth violence as an element of youth policy. The violent acts committed by a very small percentage of adolescents have become much too prominent an element in American youth policy. No greater harm can come from concern about youth violence than the creation of general policies toward children and adolescents permeated with fear and hostility. Here is the largest risk of our current youth violence debate. There is no greater protection from that ugly fate than reason, perspective, and prudent faith in the American future.

Part I

YOUTH VIOLENCE IN THE 1990s

The United States is currently experiencing the longest and one of the most intense periods of concern about youth violence in its twentieth century history. Since the early 1990s, youth violence has become a policy priority at every level of American government. Data about violent juvenile crime and statistics about the size and characteristics of the youth population are playing an important role in concerns about youth violence in the 1990s and in the first decade of the next century.

The first four chapters of this book are my attempt to provide a perspective on current concerns by marshaling the known facts about youth violence and the youth population. The first chapter is a study of attitudes about juvenile violence as they have emerged in current debates about young offenders. I contrast the ways in which youth violence was perceived in the mid-1970s with the present perception of crisis, finding many parallels and one significant distinction. The legislative response is also described.

Chapter 2 discusses basic patterns of violence during the early and middle teen years. The three key attributes of adolescent violence are pervasive group involvement, high rates of incidence, and low death rates. Such long-standing patterns are an important preliminary to chapter 3's analysis of changes since the early 1980s. As chapter 3 demonstrates, homicide and gun assaults have increased substantially. Robbery and rape have been stable. Assault and aggravated assault rates have increased, but in large measure because police are more willing to recognize many assaults as aggravated. About two-thirds of the increase in aggravated assaults are reclassifications rather than increased rates of serious violence. Under these circumstances, there is no consistent trend of youth violence to project to future years.

Chapter 4 continues the analysis of future prospects by examining trends in the youth population expected for the period 1998–2010 and measuring the known facts on population against worries about an "echo boom" of teenagers and a coming storm of juvenile crime. The total growth expected in the youth population by 2010 is a modest 19 percent. The youth population in 2010 will be equal to that of thirty years earlier, and the proportion of the total U.S. population in the teen years will be much lower in 2010 than at any time in the period between 1960 and 1980. Projections of fixed numbers of extra violent offenders, or "juvenile superpredators," are the result of logical errors about the implications of the concentration of youth arrests in delinquency research. Forecasting the coming storm of juvenile violence is science fiction, not science.

Careful analysis of past trends in youth violence and expected population changes does not produce a clear picture of the future volume of serious youth violence. High-lethality violence is a variable, low-rate event and a cyclical phenomenon among young offenders that rises and falls abruptly and without obvious explanations. The crystal ball we use to predict tomorrow's rate of serious violence is thus a very cloudy one.

But careful analysis of existing data clears away a host of half-baked statistical arguments that have dominated discourse about youth violence since the early 1990s. The good news about the coming years is that there is no scientific basis for any of the alarming predictions that are the dominant sound bites in this debate. The bad news is that all that can replace the fear mongering are healthy skepticism and caution. Most of the important influences on the rate of criminal homicide by young persons in 2010 are events that have not yet occurred.

ONE

The Perception of a Problem Is a Problem

In a series of works seldom consulted outside the academic fraternity, W. I. Thomas, the dean of American sociologists, set forth a theorem basic to the social sciences: "If men define situations as real, they are real in their consequences. . . ." The first part of the theorem provides an unceasing reminder that men respond not only to the objective features of a situation, but also, and at times primarily, to the meaning this situation has for them.

Robert K. Merton (1967)

Concern about crime and violence has remained at a high level for more than a generation in the United States. Since the early 1960s, the public's worries about crime and the political proposals in response have been consistently in the forefront of debates about the quality of American life and the capacity of government to address civic problems.

While the general problem of crime has remained consistently important, the specific focus of public and political concern has shifted in a cyclical fashion over time. At various times, the crime-related problem that is receiving priority might be urban riots, career criminals, drugs, or some other segment of the general issue. One famous recent example of this special focus on a particular subsegment of the crime problem was the war on drugs that was launched in the United States in the mid-1980s and remained the central concern in this area at least from 1985 to 1992.

The drug war is a stunning example of how periods of intense concern with particular segments of the crime problem can produce a long-lasting structural impact on government. A cabinet-level department in the national government currently coordinates a federal budget of about $15 billion as a consequence of drug war legislation, and more persons were incarcerated in federal and state prisons for drug charges by the mid-1990s than were imprisoned for all crimes twenty years earlier. Episodic concerns produce permanent consequences.

On two occasions in the past thirty years, the particular focus of public worry has turned to youth crime and youth violence. The first crisis began about 1975, in the wake of a substantial expansion in both crime rates and the youth population over the previous decade. This period lasted about three years. Its legislative impact was profound in New York State, where two separate layers of automatic transfer legislation were passed in 1976 and 1978, but more modest in most other places.

The United States is currently in the midst of its second crisis about youth crime. This time the focus is on deadly violence, on young males who carry guns and not infrequently discharge them. Concerns about youth violence came to center stage in the early 1990s. The amount of attention and legislation has remained high and shows no sign of abating.

This chapter is about perceptions of a crisis in youth violence and the ways in which they influence attitudes and government policies. The first section focuses on the contemporary description of the crisis by legislators and opinion leaders. The second section compares the most recent cycle of concern with the public's response to youth crime twenty years earlier. The third section concerns the legislative response to the perceived crisis, that is, the amount and type of legislation that current concerns have produced.

The data that are the focus of this chapter involve public opinion, descriptions of youth violence, and legislative output. No attempt will be made here to scrutinize the known facts about youth violence in order to assess the accuracy of public perceptions. The perception of crisis that is addressed is a free-standing empirical reality with many effects on government and society that do not depend on objectively measured violent acts.

"The Coming Storm"

Juvenile violence in the United States is frequently depicted as a difficult current problem that will inevitably get worse. United States Representative Bill McCollum, chair of the House Subcommittee on Crime, touches all the usual bases in testifying before a House Committee on Early Childhood, Youth, and Families in 1996:

In recent years, overall crime rates have seen a modest decline—nevertheless, this general decline masks an unprecedented surge of youth violence that has only begun to gather momentum. Today's drop in crime is only the calm before the coming storm . . .

It is important to keep in mind that [the current] dramatic increase in youth crime over the past decade occurred while the youth population was declining. Now here is that really bad news: This nation will soon have more teenagers than it has had in decades. In the final years of this decade and throughout the next, America will experience an "echo boom"—a population surge made up of the children of today's aging baby boomers. Today's enormous cohort of five year olds will be tomorrow's teenagers. This is ominous news, given that most [sic] violent crime is committed by older juveniles (those fifteen to nineteen years of age) than by any other age group. More of these youths will come from fatherless homes than ever before, at the same time that youth drug use is taking a sharp turn for the worse. *Put these demographic facts together and brace yourself for the coming generation of "super-predators."* (McCollum 1996:1–3; emphasis in original)

McCollum's statement is by no means extreme either in its rhetoric or in its substantive conclusions. It collects and repeats themes and terms quite common in the current round of alarm. His remarks will serve here as an archetypal warning about youth violence in the mid-1990s. The three themes that form the core of the statement are found in a large number of political and policy analyses. The sequence in which these themes are usually presented is this:

1. The stability or decline in rates of violence is juxtaposed against increases in rates of violent crime by young offenders.
2. It is then asserted that the volume of violent offenses will increase even more dramatically with the expected growth of the number of teenagers in the period 1995–2010 and the increases in various measures of social disadvantages among children.
3. A further increase in serious violence is regarded as all but inevitable. The argument is not usually that prudent policy can avoid the crime wave on the horizon but that "we must prepare for the coming storm of violent youth crime" (McCollum 1996:10).

These three elements can be found in a large collection of political and policy literature (e.g., DiIulio 1996, Dole 1996, Fox 1996, Wilson and Petersilia 1995). It is not the purpose of this chapter to evaluate the evidence on which these arguments rest. That is the task of chapters 2, 3, and 4. For now, it is this description of a crisis that is my central concern. How is the 1990s description of youth violence similar to that which animated public discussion in the mid-1970s? What type of legislative impact has this account of a crisis had in the states, in Congress, and in local government?

Perceptions of Youth Violence— Two Case Studies

The serious crimes committed by adolescent offenders came to be regarded as the nation's most important crime problem on two occasions separated by almost twenty years. I surveyed the discussion in the print media of the mid-1970s and mid-1990s to determine their view of the extent of crime, its causes, and its potential remedies. My reading of this written record suggests three similar themes, repeated almost verbatim in the two eras, and one important difference. The three recurrent themes are the viciousness of the new breed of offender, the revolving door of juvenile justice as a cause of crime, and the treatment of youths as adults as an attractive solution to the problem. The key difference between the two eras is the current belief that high rates of juvenile violence in the decades ahead are inevitable.

The New Breed

The first theme common to the two crises is the belief that current young offenders are *qualitatively* different from young persons who had violated the law in previous times. It is not only the number of crimes committed that has increased but also the degree of viciousness displayed by the current generation of serious offenders. The descriptions of this qualitative shift are nearly identical in the popular press of 1975 and 1995, including the use of the same rhetorical device. In 1975 *Time* tells its readers:

> The youth who are terrorizing the cities often belong to gangs, but gone are the old style rumbles with switch-blade knives and zip guns. Even criminals are frightened to work the streets in big-city areas. "I myself walk light when I am in the ghetto," says a Chicago holdup man. "I know the value of life has no weight. These younger criminals, they're sick." ("The Crime Wave" 1975)

Twenty years later, both the medium and the message are the same in *The Weekly Standard:*

> We're talking about kids that have absolutely no respect for human life and no sense of the future. . . . In a typical remark, one prisoner fretted, "I was a badass street gladiator, but these kids are stone-cold predators!" (DiIulio 1995)

The conviction that the current crop of young offenders is distinctively malevolent is important to the rhetorical case for a new policy. No matter how many additional youth crimes or young criminals are counted in a given year, the moral case for harsher punishment is better made by showing that the individual offender demands a different penal response. An account of how the individual robber, burglar, or killer is more dangerous thus meets the need of distinguishing the cases that were disposed of under traditional principles of juvenile and criminal justice; these were, after all, different and less serious offenders.

Another rhetorical function of describing the especially vicious young criminal of the new age is to present an image to the audience that is far from that of a normal adolescent. The easiest way to make a case for more punitive responses to young offenders is to completely disassociate the offenders from other youths and to disassociate the policies toward young offenders from other policies toward youths. Renaming the class being described is one method of disassociation. "Stone-cold predators" and "younger criminals" have connotative meanings quite distant from terms like "child," "youth," "adolescent," and "kid." For most citizens, it is much easier to crack down on a "younger criminal" than on a "youth."

The Revolving Door

The second part of the shared imagery of crisis in the 1970s and 1990s was the assertion that lenient treatment by the juvenile justice system was a major cause of high rates of youth crime. Two descriptions written eighteen years apart are typical:

> So many juveniles avoid arrest and prosecution that in a city like New York "the courts probably deal with less than 5 percent of the crimes against the person committed by juveniles." ("Upsurge in Violent Crime by Youngsters" 1978)

The modern day reality, critics charge, is that too many are arrested, held and released time after time in a revolving-door process that ends only if a heinous crime is committed. (Gest and Pope 1996)

The usual culprit in the "revolving door" account is the juvenile court: "Nowhere does the revolving door of justice spin faster than in the juvenile court system." Nearly one-quarter of all juvenile arrests are dismissed immediately and only 10 percent result in detention of the offender" (McNulty 1995). In this view, the central problem with revolving-door justice is its failure to restrain and deter juvenile offenders from further crime: "The kindergarten boys of today will be tomorrow's violent thugs unless America gets serious about punishing juvenile criminals" (McNulty 1995). An editorial in the *Wall Street Journal* is unqualified in its claim that leniency is a cause of violence: "Violent crime by juveniles soared in the '80s and '90s for one reason: Kids kept getting away with it" (Editorial 1997).

The arguments for harsher juvenile sanctions do not use the typical language of crime control. In the usual plea for sterner policy, terms like "general deterrence" and "incapacitation" do not appear. Instead, the key terms are "consequences for actions" and "accountability" (Senate Committee on the Judiciary 1996).

Violence as Maturity

As the last section of this chapter will show, the most common government response to a youth violence crisis is to increase the process of trying juvenile offenders in criminal courts. A legislative enthusiasm for criminal courts and adult penalties was a dominant response to fear of violence in both crime crises. The media reported both this trend and the rationale for adult treatment in very similar ways:

The current trend is to try to lower the age limit—in California from eighteen to sixteen, in Illinois from seventeen to fourteen, in New York from sixteen to fourteen—so that serious offenders can be tried like adults and be given adult penalties. ("The Crime Wave" 1975)

Nineteen years later, *Time* highlights the same strategy:

The response on the part of lawmakers has been largely to siphon the worst of them out of [the juvenile] system by lowering the age at which juveniles charged with serious crimes can be tried in adult courts. Last week in California, Governor Pete Wilson signed a bill lowering the threshold to fourteen. Earlier this year Arkansas did the same and Georgia decided that youths from the ages of fourteen through seventeen who are charged with certain crimes will be tried as adults automatically. (Lacayo 1994)

Two years later, *U.S. News and World Report* adds further examples:

The Massachusetts House of Representatives has voted to require that accused murderers as young as fourteen be tried as adults. Tennessee has eliminated any minimum age for trying some youths as adults. Oregon last year lowered its minimum age from fourteen to twelve and Wisconsin put it at ten. (Gest and Pope 1996)

The preferred position of trying youths as adults in both crisis periods had a variety of rationales. For some, it is justified solely as an instrumental method of controlling crime. If the *Wall Street Journal* assertion that juvenile crime is high only because juveniles go unpunished, then crime control is the only justification many might need for punishing very young offenders as if they were adults.

But the fact of involvement in serious crime is itself a rite of passage into adulthood, or at least evidence that the offender is no longer a child, for many advocates of adult punishment. The slogan in the 1990s is "If you're old enough to do the crime, you're old enough to do the time." Although the logic behind this message is not self-evident, its appeal is not solely to retributive instincts. The notion instead is that serious violence is not a characteristic behavior of childhood—that violence is somehow adult.

The Virginia Governor's Commission on Juvenile Justice (1995) puts this sort of argument in specific terms:

Virginia's juvenile justice system was not intended to cope with serious, violent offenders. Constructed in the 1970s, it was designed to deal largely with vandalism and childish pranks. The system reflects an indulgent attitude that juvenile crime should not be referred to as "crime"; that juvenile wrongdoers, even those juveniles who commit violent crimes such as murder, rape and robbery, should be adjudged "delinquent" rather than "guilty." (p. 3)

Readers will note that the good old days of vandalism and pranks in this account are the same period in the mid-1970s that produced the first postwar youth crime crisis. To hear this era referred to as an innocent age is much like hearing the holdup man, complaining in 1995 about the "stone-cold predators" now on the street, contrast these feral beasts with the less violent crew of his youth, presumably around 1975.

The Emergence of Categorical Determinism

The most striking contrast between the 1970s crisis and that of the 1990s concerns the type of worries about the future and the evident theories of the causes of youth crime. There was, to begin, less emphasis on likely future developments in the 1970s—things were bad enough in the present for even the most pessimistic observers. If conditions in 1975 cast shadows over the future, it was the fear of the future development of current young offenders. If the then current cohort of 15-year-olds had more than its share of nasty characters, the same bad dispositions that created special trouble in their teen years should also cause larger than usual problems in early adulthood. This is one variety of what sociologists call a *cohort phenomenon*—a natural outgrowth of worries that the youth population of the present had more than its share of major offenders.

The crime crisis of the 1990s placed much more emphasis on future trends than the earlier crisis, but the heavy emphasis was not put on the cohort effects to be expected as the 1990s generation of 15-year-olds grew up. The major problem of coming decades was not the future activities of today's youth but rather the trouble that would probably arise from the larger group of adolescents expected in the United States in the period between 2000 and 2010. Thus, Representative McCollum (1996) tells his colleagues that current conditions are only the calm before the coming storm.

The numerical basis for this concern is a projected increase in the adolescent population from the relatively low levels of 1990 and 1995. But how do we know whether and to what extent the teens of 2010 are likely to commit serious crimes of violence? Those who worried in 1975 that a group of adolescents aged 15 to 18 who have higher than average rates of violent crime might continue to cause above-average trouble based their concerns on the demonstrated propensities of a population group that already has a track record for misbehavior. The extent of cohort effects is difficult to estimate because predicting future behavior from past conduct is a tricky business. But a projection of future trends based on past conduct is not a novel or shocking element of social theory.

The mid-1990s predictions of major crime explosions are not based on the demonstrated propensities of a population group. The teenagers of 2010 were either unborn in 1995 or under 4 years of age. Believing them to be almost certainly a coming storm of juvenile violence must imply that the causes of serious juvenile violence are fixed and objective circumstances, such as the number of children in a population group, family status, place of residence, and other characteristics determined at a very early age. Only a rather extreme version of a deterministic view of the causes of juvenile violence can give support to the notion that homicide rates fifteen years in the future can be predicted for a group of children currently between 2 and 4 years old. So talk about "270,000 juvenile superpredators coming at us in waves" in 2010 depends on a belief in fixed relationships between population characteristics and rates of serious violence.

Two further points merit mention. As a tactical matter, the threat of future crisis might be thought necessary to attract public attention during a period when crime and violence are going down. As a political tactic, predicting a future crime wave in 2010 is almost riskless, if only because predictions fifteen years in the future do not often haunt those in political life.

As a strategic matter, however, arguing that the later course of criminal careers can be predicted long in advance seems inconsistent with doctrines of free will and moral accountability, which are important to the case for adult punishment and responsibility. The term "stone-cold predator" seems designed for persons who elect to violate the law when a life of crime might easily be avoided. Yet long-range predictions of juvenile behavior work well only if the outcome of choices between criminal and noncriminal life styles is highly predictable. There seems to be substantial tension between predicting with confidence that newborn babies in bad neighborhoods will produce a fixed quota of street predators and putting the full weight of moral blame that animates the machinery of criminal punishment on the products of this predetermined process.

Legislative Responses

The climate of concern in the early 1990s has produced a bumper crop of legislative responses at every level of government. Indeed, the most striking characteristic of the years since 1992 has been the universality of legislative responses to the youth crime crisis. New youth violence laws were not passed in just some states or in many states but in virtually all the states in the federal union from 1992 to 1997. Moreover, new federal statutes and legal proposals ran the gamut from "gun-free schools" to an omnibus package of crime, gang, and gun proposals submitted by President Clinton in 1997. County and city governments with no direct criminal code responsibilities have nonetheless passed curfew ordinances, antigang laws, and other regulatory measures as local contributions to the paper war on youth violence.

The universal urge to legislate during the 1990s suggests a model of legal reform that is disturbing. If all the states revise juvenile and criminal justice provisions during a crime crisis, the inference is that the real motive for legislation is discomfort with levels of youth violence rather than with particular flaws in how young offenders are processed or the identification of specific improvements in court or correctional processes. Legislation becomes the result of a felt need to do something about crime, a need that may be totally external to the operations of legal systems that respond to juvenile and late adolescent violence.

The apparent assumption that has been driving legislation in the 1990s is that high rates of youth violence must mean that the legal institutions that deal with violence are deficient. The reasoning behind this assumption is far from impeccable. If advocates suggested that an increase in homicide rates proved that the criminal courts were failures in the adjudication and sentencing of murder, both their logic and their qualifications as policy analysts would be challenged. Criminal courts cope with homicide after the fact and cannot be expected to prevent most crimes from occurring. Homicide rates go up and down for many reasons beyond the control of courts or the legal system. It would thus be irrational to the point of superstition to base judgments about the efficacy of criminal courts on fluctuations in homicide rates.

But that sort of superstitious belief seems to be an important element in assuming that high rates of adolescent violence must require major changes in the legal framework. Legislative changes that are based solely on concern about high offense rates are vulnerable to error in a special way. As long as a proponent of legislative change has the burden of demonstrating a malfunction in the current system before attempting an untested remedy, changes can be confined to problems in the system that need to be addressed. This does not guarantee that a proposed remedy will work, of course. Eric Severeid once suggested that "the chief cause of problems is solutions" (Silberman 1978:169)—all the more reason to believe that instituting changes without identifying problems is a very risky venture.

Varieties of Recent Reforms

Whereas the specific forms of legislative intervention have varied widely in the 1990s, the basic theme of the current era is getting tough. There is, of course, nothing novel in getting tough as a mode of criminal justice legislation. The rhetoric of toughness is always popular in crime policy, particularly when citizens are frightened. But there is one further reason why aggression must be the key symbol in the 1990s legislative reforms. If the motivation for legislative change is the need to reduce crime, some theory about new policies will differ from the (presumed) inefficiency of previous polices is required. The new regime must be characterized as active rather than passive, an act of government that can be interposed somehow to prevent the next serious crime wave from occurring. Government policy must be seen to have this kind of aggressive thrust because the purpose of reform is not the better functioning of a legal process but stopping crime. In other words, the imagery of aggression is necessary to the symbolic function of fighting crime.

Yet the rhetoric of toughness can be adapted to many different types of legal change. Longer sentences for young offenders in juvenile or criminal courts is one obvious version of getting tough on youth violence. So are gun-free schools and special criminal enforcement for interdicting firearms that might be available to the young, as well as special federal, state, and local antigang strike forces. All must clothe themselves in the mantle of toughness, and all must present some story of crime prevention, either by the removal of youths before they can reoffend or the destruction of a violent gang framework or the interception of a handgun headed for street use.

Of all the get-tough methods advocated in the 1990s, the most popular state legislation has been increasing the sanctions for violent crimes committed by young persons below the maximum age of juvenile court jurisdiction, usually by transferring these juveniles into the jurisdiction and full penalties of the criminal courts. One state-by-state analysis reported that forty-seven states have increased sanctions on juvenile acts of violence (Snyder and Sickmund 1995). In forty states, transfer is possible for new crimes or for a younger offender or at the discretion of a prosecutor, who might choose whether to file for the most serious charge without a judge's final authority (Snyder and Sickmund 1995).

Laws that selectively increase transfers into criminal courts have advantages over other methods of getting tough that range from low cost to high symbolic value. Even state laws that provide for automatic criminal court jurisdiction of serious acts of violence like homicide and rape will not carry a price tag that is either large or immediate. The number of cases turn out to be small, and local prosecutors may avoid transfer by not filing a charge for a crime that makes it automatic; moreover, so many previous laws have created transfer opportunities that using this strategy requires few innovations in legislative drafting. Thus waiver provisions are fighting youth crime on the cheap.

The symbolic value of transfer to criminal courts is that it seems to completely resolve the conflict that many citizens feel when very young adolescents are charged with serious acts of violence. The conflict is between the impulse to punish criminals, on the one hand, and to protect children and youths, on the other. Transfer to adult court resolves this conflict by declaring the defendant to be no longer a child. In specific cases in which a particular youth and a particular crime are in public view, this sort of legerdemain may have limited value. But at the legislative level, the general proclamation that all who are charged with the commission of a particular crime should be regarded as adults removes by definition the ambivalence that is characteristic of reactions to violence by the very young.

A second form of getting tough that has had significant support in the 1990s is the expansion of punishment power in the juvenile court past legal adulthood. This strategy has been called "blended jurisdiction" in recent years. Some states have created these enhancements as alternatives to transferring young offenders into criminal courts. In Massachusetts, for example, the young offenders eligible for long sentences in special juvenile courts are not eligible for waiver into criminal courts except when charged with first or second degree murder. In Texas, however, juveniles can be waived under some circumstances and are subject to penalty enhancements under others. In these systems, blended jurisdiction should be regarded as a supplement to waiver rather than a substitute. An exact count of jurisdictions that have such significantly expanded punishments is difficult to determine, but fewer than ten comprehensive systems are in place now and not all of them use the court's new powers frequently.

These new forms of juvenile court are legally novel and complex, in contrast to transfer to criminal courts.

The symbolic content of blended jurisdiction is variable. Expanding penalties is, of course, a common way of getting tough, so the process can be sold as punitive. But when viewed as an alternative to criminal court transfer, it can be seen as a way to avoid the excommunication of the young defendant from the juvenile system. This holding on to the status of juvenile often has an important symbolic value.

A third set of very common legislative changes has altered the conditions and consequences of juvenile court delinquency proceedings. This objective is to deprive delinquency proceedings of some of the special protections that separated delinquency in the juvenile court from criminal adjudication. The most frequent target of this type of change in the 1990s has been the nonpublic nature of juvenile court proceedings and records. More than three-quarters of the states have allowed more public access to proceedings or records or both (Snyder and Sickmund 1995). The symbolic content is in removing the privileged status that is the presumed cause of high rates of juvenile violence.

Whereas all the state-level reforms discussed have the juvenile offender as their principal target, two other components of the new imagery of youth violence are guns and gangs. Gun use by juveniles accounted for over 90 percent of the increase in juvenile homicide over 1985–1992 (Zimring 1996). The surge in gun violence presented a target for getting tough that was more in keeping with traditional liberal sentiments than wholesale transfer of juveniles to criminal courts. In short order, the 1990s witnessed a federal gun-free schools act, state laws making handgun possession by minors either prohibited or more severely punished, and a variety of special enforcement efforts from federal and local police that were directed at juvenile gun possession and use. Special laws and law enforcement efforts directed toward juvenile gangs have also been frequent since 1991, and even the Federal Bureau of Investigation (FBI) has created special youth gang staffing and programs.

How Much Change?

Almost certainly, the years since 1991 have witnessed a larger volume of legislation on the subject of adolescent violence than any previous short period. But the scale of the changes wrought by all this legislation is easy to exaggerate. What has not been changed in the legislative frenzy of the 1990s is as noteworthy as what has. It is important to note that the authority and jurisdiction of the juvenile courts in delinquency cases have not been significantly narrowed in any state. Many more jurisdictions made punitive changes in waiver provisions in the 1990s than during the crisis of the mid-1970s, but none of these changes in recent years cut nearly as deeply into the jurisdiction and authority of a juvenile court as did the New York State legislation of 1976 and 1978 (Singer 1996) or the Florida legislation of 1983 (Bishop and Frazier 1991). In the 1990s, significant reductions in juvenile court delinquency caseloads are not even talking points of mainstream political constituencies in most proposed legislation. The court itself is much criticized, but its hegemony in dealing with the violent acts of younger adolescents has not been challenged.

The only loss of legal power associated with the flurry of legislation in the current era is the shift from judicial to prosecutorial power in transferring a case to criminal court. The expansion of punishment power associated with blended jurisdiction increases the work load of the juvenile court but is no diminution of its authority. If the reforms of the past decade are typical of future trends, it is the mission of the juvenile court rather than its jurisdiction that is at risk. The goal of punitive reforms has been to reorient the juvenile court rather than to cut back on its size, its influence, or its power. For those who support the traditional missions of juvenile justice, the biggest worry will be not the decline in power of the juvenile court but the new policies that a powerful juvenile justice system may soon serve.

American Youth Violence—
A Profile

Chapter 1 is about perceptions of youth violence in the United States. This chapter and chapter 3 are about the facts. What sorts of violence do young persons commit in the United States? How are these violent acts measured and with what margins of error? How are rates of violence distributed across the youth population? How are patterns of youth violence similar to patterns of adult violence, and how are they different? What have been the trends in recent history for various kinds of violence?

The analysis is presented under three headings. The first part of this chapter discusses the different acts that are classified as violent and how they are measured by police agencies and survey researchers. Rates of different types of violence are reported by age, race, and gender. The second part distinguishes three characteristics that set young violent offenders apart from other violent offenders: group involvement, high volume, and low lethality. To develop policy for youth violence, the special nature of the crimes must be understood. Chapter 3 builds on this discussion to chart trends over time in official statistics on youth violence, the third part of our profile.

Classification and Measurement

Two sources of information are available about the incidence and character of youth violence in the United States—official statistics from police departments and survey research estimates from interviews with samples of the population.

Police statistics are limited to the cases in which the age of the offender has been determined, so the only official statistics on youth violence in the United States are data about arrests. For the majority of all offenses, for which no suspect is identified, there is no indication of the offender's age. One way around this problem is to estimate the share of total crime attributable to young offenders by assuming that the percentage of their violent crime arrests is also the percentage of all violent crimes they commit. Even if a small minority of all robberies are cleared by arrest, why not assume that since juveniles account for 32 percent of all robbery arrests, they also account for 32 percent of all robberies?

This is the most frequent method used to establish the proportion of violent acts attributable to young offenders, but it results in an overestimate. Younger offenders commit offenses in groups much more often than older offenders, and they are also arrested in groups much more often. If four 16-year-olds are arrested for one burglary and one 24-year-old is arrested for one burglary, the young offenders are responsible for half the crimes (one out of two) but 80 percent of the arrests (four out of five). Furthermore, if very young offenders are less skilled at evading capture, they will constitute a larger fraction of all arrests than their percentage of the total criminal population. It is well established that group arrests lead to a bias that overstates the amount of violence committed by young offenders (Reiss 1986; Zimring 1981). Whether a higher clearance rate when youths commit particular crimes exacerbates this problem is not known. Whereas the bias may be substantial at any given time, it is not known whether changes over time in group arrest proportions also invalidate this measure.

Types of Offenses

Five crime categories reported by the police involve the immediate threat or imposition of injury to the person: homicide, rape, aggravated assault, robbery, and assault. The homicide category covers cases in which death is caused by the willful (nonnegligent) killing of one human being by another (U.S. Department of Justice, Federal Bureau of Investigation 1995:13). The technical label of this category is murder and nonnegligent manslaughter. There were 21,597 such cases in 1995. Arrests under the age of 21 accounted for 37 percent of all homicide arrests; arrests under the age of 18 accounted for 15 percent.

Forcible rape is defined as the completed or attempted act of sexual intercourse accomplished by force or the threat of imminent force. A total of 97,464 rapes were reported by the Uniform Crime Reports in 1995. Offenders under 21 made up 28 percent of all rape arrests in 1995; offenders under 18 were involved in 16 percent of all rape arrests.

Aggravated assault is an unlawful attack by one person on another for the purpose of inflicting severe or aggravated bodily injury. This type of assault is usually accompanied by use of a weapon or by means likely to produce death or great bodily harm (U.S. Department of Justice, Federal Bureau of Investigation, 1995:31). There were 1,099,179 such assaults reported in 1995, or fifty-one times the volume of homicide. Offenders under 21 made up 26 percent of all arrests in 1995; offenders under 18 were involved in 15 percent. The category of aggravated assault does not require either a wounding or a shot fired if attack by a deadly weapon was threatened, so aggravated assaults range in seriousness from menacing gestures to attempted murder.

Robbery is taking or attempting to take anything of value from the care, custody, or control of a person by force or by threat of force or violence or by putting the victim in fear (U.S. Department of Justice, Federal Bureau of Investigation, 1995:26). There were 580,545 reported robberies in 1995. Offenders under 21 made up 51 percent of robbery arrests; offenders under 18 made up 32 percent of all arrests. Robbery is another category that includes acts with a wide range of peril, from schoolyard extortions to armed invasions of banks. Thus, the general category is heterogeneous. Just knowing the crime category does not tell much about how life-threatening were the specific acts reported.

Assaults are the Uniform Crime Report category for attacks that fail to meet the criteria for aggravated assault but are still regarded as criminal. Because most life-threatening attacks are upgraded to the aggravated category, the residual assault classification usually involves attacks that were not life-threatening. This less serious classification is not a Part I or Index offense in the Uniform Crime Reporting Program, which is the highest priority classification in the Federal Bureau of Investigation program, and assault statistics are frequently not included in the analysis of violent crime, despite the fact that many nonaggravated assaults involve more injury to the victim than many robberies.

There is one final offense now reported in the Index with the potential for personal injury, the crime of arson. This is a relatively new entry, with extreme heterogeneity, which will be excluded from the analysis in this study.

Offense Seriousness and Frequency

The five police-reported categories of violent crime can be broken down into three categories. First, homicide and forcible rape are crimes of high seriousness. If an offense is properly classified into one of these two categories, the observer knows that the criminal harm was substantial. Second, robbery and aggravated assault are heterogeneous offense categories. Many assaults are only a fraction of an inch or a quick ambulance trip away from murder, but many other aggravated assaults are far less serious. The same great range is found in robberies. Third, nonaggravated assault, in contrast, is an offense of lower seriousness.

Figure 2.1 shows the distribution of youth arrests by type of crime for 1995.

The pattern is similar for both younger and older adolescents but more pronounced in the younger groups. For offenders under 18, a

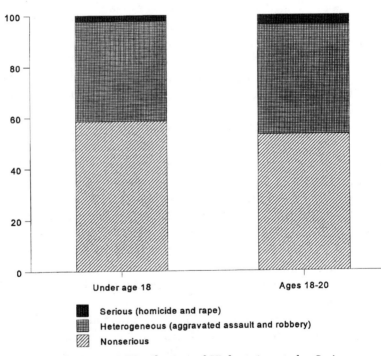

Figure 2.1. Percentage Distribution of Violent Arrests by Seriousness of Crime, 1995. Source: U.S. Department of Justice, Federal Bureau of Investigation (1995).

majority of all violence arrests is for the nonserious offense of assault. The next large cluster of offenses is the heterogeneous group. Aggravated assault and robbery are a mixed bag of life-threatening and less serious events. Fewer than 2 percent of all violent offenses for those under 18 involve the always serious crimes of homicide and rape. Ninety-eight percent of all violence arrests and more than 95 percent of the arrests for the more serious Part I violent crimes are for some forms of assault and robbery.

For 18- to 20-year-olds, the concentration at the low end of the seriousness scale is slightly less pronounced. Homicide and rape arrests account for under 5 percent of the total violence arrests in the 18-to-20 age group and about 10 percent of the age group arrests for the four Part I offenses of violence, about twice the concentration found for the younger group. Nonserious assault is still the largest of the three categories, followed closely by the heterogeneous aggravated assaults and robberies.

The data in figure 2.1 do not lead to any confident conclusions about the seriousness of youth violence in the United States in the mid-1990s. Arrests for the most serious categories are small, but many thousands of the aggravated assault and robbery arrests may result from very serious forms of these offenses. This cannot be investigated in the aggregated crime statistics. A wide variety of different levels of seriousness are found in the young offenders apprehended and in the offenses they commit.

The Demography of Youth Violence

The data compiled from arrest statistics can be used to estimate the degree to which arrest rates vary for different subpopulations of American youths. The key variables that differentiate arrest risk are age, gender, and race.

Figure 2.2 uses 1995 arrest data and census-based population projections to estimate arrest rates by age for the four Part I offenses of violence. Homicide and rape arrest rates are multiplied by ten to create spatial continuity. The propensity to be arrested for violent crimes begins low and increases steadily through the midteens. The peak rate is at age 18 for all offenses except robbery, which peaks at 17. For homicide, the rate at 18 is ten times the rate at 13 and 14, and the peak rate for the other three offenses is about two and one-half times the rate of arrests at 13 and 14. The drop-off after 18 is modest for all offenses other than robbery, but it is almost 40 percent for robbery.

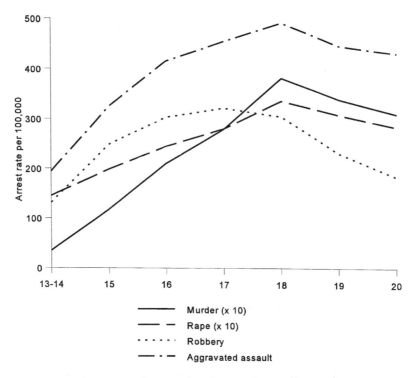

Figure 2.2. Arrest Rates by Age for Four Violent Offenses 1995. Source: U.S. Department of Justice, Federal Bureau of Investigation (1995).

The arrest statistics show some increase with age in heterogeneous offenses of robbery and aggravated assault. What is not knowable from these data is whether there is a progression in the assault and robbery categories with advancing age toward the more life-threatening types of the offenses. The sharp increase in homicide rates from ages 13 and 14 to age 18 suggests that there is such a progression.

The concentration of violent crime among males is a familiar tale, told in these statistics by figure 2.3. For each of the three age groups in the figure, the male-to-female ratio is computed by assuming a fifty-fifty gender split in the population. Rape is omitted from the analysis. Males dominate arrests for violent crime for every category at every age; the male-to-female arrest ratios are never lower than four to one. This male dominance is well known. What is more surprising is the tendency for male-to-female arrests to be markedly higher during the adolescent years for homicide and robbery. The homicide arrests of males are fifteen times those of females under the age of 18 and more than sixteen times the female level at ages 18 to 20. This is twice the male-to-female ratio noted in adulthood. The male-to-female ratios for younger offenders in robbery are also significantly higher than the gender ratio for adults. It is only for assault that younger male offenders are not pronouncedly more numerous.

The most plausible explanation for the hyperconcentration of younger males in the arrest statistics is that the cultural forces that push male rates to extreme levels during adolescence do not operate in that fashion for females. It is not a dearth of female offenders that drives the male-to-female arrest ratios so high in the midteens; it is the peak incidence of male violence that is the only moving part. Female rates of homicide and robbery are relatively flat. When the male rates come down somewhat, the male-to-female ratios come down as well.

Figure 2.4 adds a final dimension to the distribution of arrests by

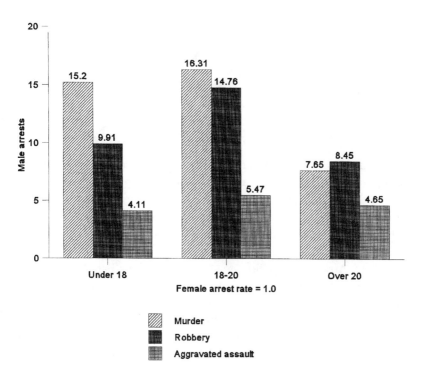

Figure 2.3. Ratio of Male Arrests as a Multiple of Female Arrests for Three Violent Crimes, 1995. Source: U.S. Department of Justice, Federal Bureau of Investigation (1995).

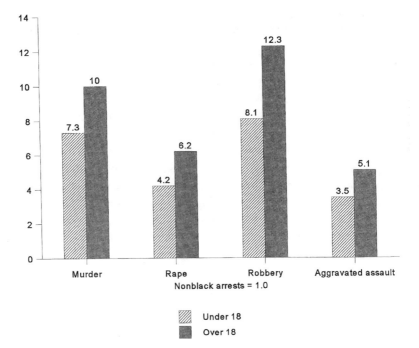

Figure 2.4. Ratio of Black Arrests as a Multiple of Nonblack Arrests, by Offense and Age Group, 1995. Source: U.S. Department of Commerce, Bureau of the Census (1995b); U.S. Department of Justice, Federal Bureau of Investigation (1995).

expressing the African-American arrest rate for Part I violent crimes as a percentage of the arrest rate for all the other groups. The two age groups in the analysis are under the age of 18 (whose arrests are compared to the population aged 13 to 17) and over the age of 18 (for whom the adult population is used as the base).

The data reported in figure 2.4 show substantially higher rates of arrest for African Americans for each of the four Part I offenses of violence for both juvenile and adult age groups. The concentrations are highest for robbery and homicide and lowest for aggravated assault. This pattern has been noted previously, with the concentration of African-American arrests much larger for violent offenses than for property crimes (Zimring and Hawkins 1997). What is novel in the pattern of figure 2.4 is that the ratio of African-American arrests is significantly higher for each offense among adults than among 13- to

17-year-olds, the under-18 population having high rates of violence. The racial concentration of homicide arrests is 37 percent higher for adults than for juveniles, and the adult figures for the other three crimes are about 50 percent greater in the ratio of black to nonblack arrest rates than for juveniles. The rape concentration is 45 percent higher among adults, the robbery concentration is 52 percent higher, and the assault concentration is 45 percent higher.

The most plausible explanation for the lower levels of racial concentration in comparisons for juveniles is that the greater male prevalence of violence during adolescence means that larger numbers of males of all ethnic groups are exposed to arrest, and this reduces the intense overrepresentation of African Americans. The reduced concentration is most apparent in the two heterogeneous violence offenses—robbery and aggravated assault. The arrest concentration among African Americans is lowest in aggravated assaults (at 3.5 in ages 13 to 17), precisely where a larger rate of assaultive violence among all boys would be expected to most depress the racial concentration of arrests. For nonaggravated assaults, the racial concentration of arrests dropped to 2.8 for juveniles, the only value under 3.00 in violent offenses. The much higher concentration of juvenile homicide arrests among blacks than of aggravated assault arrests (7.3 to 3.5) is some evidence that less life-threatening assaults are more evenly spread across the adolescent male population than are attacks likely to cause death or great bodily harm.

Survey-based Rate Estimates

The data in figures 2.2, 2.3, and 2.4 all come from police arrest statistics, which generate biases that are both substantial and obvious. For some time, sociologists have been asking large samples of young persons about their self-reported criminal activities; the statistical estimates generated by these surveys provide an independent measure of the incidence of violence among young persons and the distribution of violence in the youth population. The contrast between survey estimates and police statistics is clear—the surveys estimate much higher levels of violence and more youth participation in violent acts. At the same time, the self-report studies show much less concentration among high-risk, urban, minority males. To move from police statistics and cohort analyses based on police data into the self-reported crimes of the national youth studies is to enter a world where there are many more assaults and where fighting is more evenly spread across the population.

To ask which of these two portraits of youth violence is the correct one may miss the central point of the comparison. Each strategy may be accurate in its measurements, but each is measuring different types and intensities of violent behavior. The sample surveys and panel studies report extensive levels of adolescent male participation in violent conduct, but the great majority of these acts are clustered at the less serious end of the distribution of assaults and robberies. The arrest statistics reflect violent acts that have been screened for seriousness first by the victims (who may not report attacks to the police) and then by the police. These more serious cases are more concentrated in minority, male population groups.

It is, therefore, possible to accommodate the different portraits of adolescent violence that emerge from official statistics and survey research. It would be unwise to assume, however, that all of the assaultive behavior measured by surveys is other than life-threatening. Little is known about the number of serious cases of assault and robbery that are not referred to the police, in large part because the adolescent victims did not report them. Whereas homicide cases are quite difficult to conceal, very serious but not fatal violent acts are often undercounted. We need only remember the reporting and treatment of rape cases in the recent past to understand the potential of official statistics to conceal a large, dark figure of unreported serious violence.

But the homicide statistics tell us that unreported acts of life-threatening violence may also be concentrated in the same populations that dominate the current official statistics. If current homicide cases provide an accurate index of where the most serious adolescent violence is located, the problem may be larger than the official statistics suggest but is probably concentrated in the same social locations as currently observed homicide cases.

Distinctive Characteristics of Youth Violence

Three features of the violent acts committed by adolescent offenders distinguish youth violence from that of older age groups: high volume, low mortality, and group involvement. These characteristics interact to produce a behavioral profile sharply different from violence at other life stages.

High Volume

Rates of participation in violence by adolescent boys are much higher than for males of any other age. Figure 2.5 shows reported rates of victimization for the three peak age groups, early adolescence, midadolescence, and the transition years to young adulthood. The rates in the figure are per thousand youths per year for assault and per 100,000 per year for homicide. The data reported are for victimization, which is also a good measure of offense rates at least where conflict-motivated assaults among age peers are widespread.

The highest rates involve 16- to 19-year-old boys: One out of ten reports being assaulted each year. The next-youngest and next-oldest groups are tied for second place in victimization, with annual victimization rates of 7.5 percent. In another study, when young men are asked about their participation in serious fights, about one-quarter report behavior that would meet the standards for criminal assault (Elliott and Menard 1996).

A large proportion of young men participate in violence at some point during youth—the high rate of what epidemiologists call the prevalence of violence in adolescence. If a male will ever be involved in violence, adolescence is when it will happen. A corollary is that the majority of those who do participate in violence during adolescence do not report violent behavior later on in adulthood. Three-quarters of those who report adolescent violence in a recent study (Elliott 1994) do not report any later violence. Psychologists differentiate between those who are involved in violence during adolescence only and those they call "life course persisters." The social settings and pressures of adolescence thus create the high-water mark for the involvement of otherwise normal boys in violent conflict.

Whether and to what extent adolescence-only violence includes the most life-threatening forms or is restricted to the less serious forms of assault is an important issue not definitively addressed in currently available research. Are there environments and circumstances where adolescence-only offenders carry guns or use lethal weapons? If so what are these circumstances?

Low Mortality

The second distinctive feature of American youth violence makes the very high rates of violence less frightening as a matter of public health. Despite the high levels of violent attacks in adolescence, the

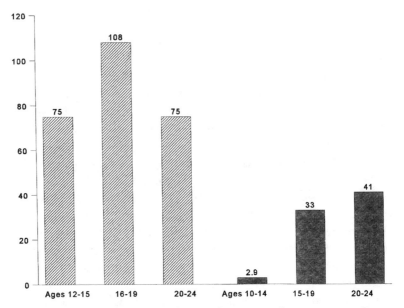

Figure 2.5. Male Homicide and Assault Victims, by Age, 1991. Source: National Center for Health Statistics (1991:36); U.S. Department of Justice, Bureau of Justice Statistics (1991:24, Table 5).

death rate from adolescent violence is much lower than the death rate from violent assaults of adults. The three rightmost columns in figure 2.5 show homicide rates for three age categories that nearly match the age groups reported on the left for assault. For the youngest age group, there are more than 2,500 reported assaults for every homicide; for the next oldest group, there are 327 assaults per homicide; for the 20- to 24-age groups, the ratio is 187 to 1. Both 12- to 15-year-olds and 20- to 24-year-olds reported assault victimization rates of 7.5 per 100 during 1991, but the homicide rate for the older group is fourteen times as high as for the younger group.

A series of factors contribute to this low death rate. Most teenagers are hard targets, unlikely to die from attacks with ordinary personal force or blunt objects. This distinguishes teens from very young children, who are more vulnerable to beatings, but not from young adults. The use of guns and knives in adolescent fights is lower than for young adults in reported violent assaults. This seems to be the major difference between the midteens and the mid-20s.

Group Involvement

The third distinguishing feature of adolescent violence is high rates of group involvement. For young persons under 16, data collected in the Vera Institute Family Court study (Zimring 1981) suggests that the majority of all persons charged with violent offenses committed the offense with one or more co-offenders, as shown in figure 2.6.

The high group involvement in violence is paralleled by high group involvement in all crimes during the same life stage. Whatever youths are doing in their teens, they are doing it in groups. The percentage of group involvement in crime is much lower in adulthood (Zimring 1981). The high rate of group involvement provides a different context for youth violence and also suggests that the motives for violent behavior may be different in group settings. This matter is addressed in some detail in chapter 5.

Two aspects of the data in figure 2.6 require preliminary comment. First, the estimate of group involvement is conservative in one signi-

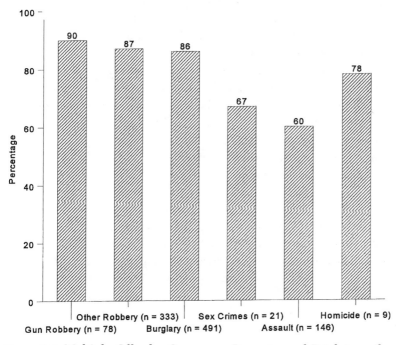

Figure 2.6. Multiple Offender Cases as a Percentage of Total Juveniles Charged, by Crime, New York City. Source: Zimring (1981).

ficant respect. A co-offender was noted in this study only if he or she was apprehended. When only one burglar or thief was caught, the offense is not listed as a group enterprise. This surely undercounts the extent of group involvement. Second, this was a study of New York delinquents, so only offenders under 16 are represented. Older adolescents probably commit more offenses alone, although we do not yet have any detailed data on the relationship between age and group offenses in adolescence.

Thus, the data in figure 2.6 tell us that most 14- and 15-year-old law violators, no matter what their crime, are committing the offense with others. This group context is frequently the most important element in explaining the nature of a particular offense and why a particular offender is involved. The immediate motive for criminal involvement is group standing. The participant is showing off, living up to group expectations, pressing to avoid being ridiculed. The common characteristic of these motives is that they are loosely tied to the particular objective of the substantive criminal offense. Group standing is probably the central concern of the adolescent offender in group crime, and the message of figure 2.6 may be that group standing is the central concern for most youthful offenders, regardless of the particular criminal violation involved. This is one plausible explanation for the universality of high group involvement in the crimes of early adolescence.

Since group involvement plays a much smaller role in the criminal behavior of older offenders, its dominance in adolescent crime tells us that an important transition is likely between adolescence and later life, whether or not there is persistence in criminal behavior. The offender will make a transition either to noncriminal behavior or to criminal behavior with different motives and no co-offenders. Either change is of obvious significance.

All of the preceding discussion is a necessary foundation to the task of the next chapter. Chapter 3 shows the importance of understanding the definition and measurement of common violent offenses in comprehending the recent changes in youth violence in the United States.

THREE

A Youth Violence Epidemic
Myth or Reality?

Current concerns about youth violence policy have been driven by interpretations of official statistics on youth arrests, as noted in chapter 1. Arrest statistics have been quoted as proof of substantial increases in the violence attributable to young offenders. These statistics have then been used as evidence that a new and more vicious breed of juvenile offender is the reason for the increase in arrests. Finally, predictions about future rates of youth violence have been based on projecting recent trends many years in the future.

This chapter is a detailed analysis of recent trends in arrest statistics. The first section examines trends in the four Part I or Index offenses of violence over the period 1980–1996. The second section focuses on youth arrests for homicide, concluding that the increase noted in this category is attributable to increases in gun violence. The third section shows that arrests for aggravated assault—the largest growth category since 1980—may be the result of changes in police practices and reporting standards. A concluding section addresses the implications of the statistical patterns revealed in this chapter in projecting rates of youth crime.

A General Trend?

As discussed in chapter 2, the only official statistics that provide age-specific patterns are police data on arrests. These are the statistics that have been the basis for predictions of a coming wave of youth violence. Figure 3.1 combines national-level data on arrests under the age of 18 with census-based data on age to present trends on arrest rates per 100,000 youths aged 13 to 17 for homicide, rape, aggravated assault, and robbery. For each offense, the arrest rate per 100,000 in 1980 is expressed as a baseline level of 100, and each

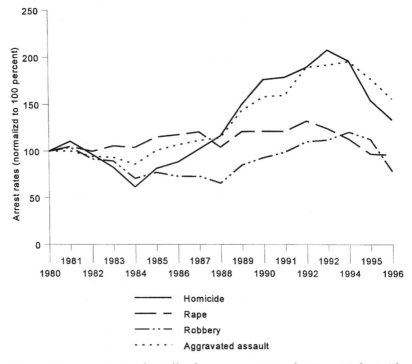

Figure 3.1. Arrest Rates for Offenders, Ages 13–17, for Four Violent Offenses, 1980–1996. Source: U.S. Department of Justice, Federal Bureau of Investigation (1980–1993, 1994a, 1995–1996).

succeeding year's arrest rate is expressed as a percentage of that figure. This graph shows trends in all four offense categories most directly.

The estimates generated in figure 3.1 express the number of arrests over the entire population of 13- to 17-year-olds despite the fact that the percentage of the U.S. population in reporting agencies varies and is never 100 percent. Thus the rates derived are an index of trends rather than a precise rate.

Two of the four offenses show pronounced trends over time— homicide and aggravated assault. The largest movements over time are noted for homicide, for which the arrest rate first dropped by just under 40 percent in the early 1980s and then began a sustained climb after 1984. The peak rate in 1993 was more than double the 1980 level. Then homicide arrests dropped sharply; the 1996 rate was 34 percent above that in 1980. The arrest level for aggravated assault did not drop much in the early 1980s and then increased slowly from 1985 to 1988. Large one-year jumps in 1989 and again in 1992 raised the level to nearly double the 1980 rate. The rate declined by 20 percent over the two years after its 1994 peak, but arrests for aggravated assault stayed 56 percent above the 1980 level, by far the largest increase in the four violent crimes.

Trends in rape and robbery arrests over the 1980s and early 1990s were much less pronounced. Rape arrests never dropped lower than their 1980 baseline during the years, the early 1980s, when homicide and assault declined. Rape arrest rates increased after 1988, reaching a high 32 percent above the 1980 level in 1992, but dropped back by 1996 to the lowest rate recorded at any time since 1977.

Robbery arrest trends differ from the others in two respects. While arrest rates for other violent crimes went up after 1984, robbery arrests declined in six of the first eight years of the 1980s and reached their lowest level of the 1980s in 1988. From 1988 to 1994, the arrest rates increased but were never more than 20 percent above the 1980 baseline. The 1995 rate dropped to 13 percent above the 1980 rate, and the 1996 arrest rate fell another 34 percent. By 1996, the robbery arrest rate was reported at 21 percent below the 1980 level.

There are three notable elements in the aggregate pattern reported in figure 3.1. First, there is no common pattern for youth arrests for violent crime during the 1980–1996 period. The rate change over the sixteen-year period ranges from −21 percent for robbery to +56 percent for aggravated assault. Homicide, which had the highest increase as recently as 1993, recorded a 34 percent gain by the end of 1996. The four different offenses are thus four different statistical stories.

The second major conclusion is that youth violence arrest rates usually do not run up or down in long cycles. In a period that was supposed to be noteworthy because of its sustained upward trends, only three times did the arrest rate go in the same direction for an offense for more than three consecutive years. Two of the four offenses of violence were essentially trendless over the sixteen years in the aggregate.

The third important characteristic is that the arrest rate often changes substantially in a short time. Over the sixteen year-to-year transitions in figure 3.1, homicide rates increased or decreased by over 20 percent in four years and over 15 percent a total of seven times. Aggravated assault rates recorded one-year increases of 34 percent, 19 percent, and 17 percent in the sixteen year-to-year changes.

The volatility of trends in arrests means that rates of offenses—which cannot be predicted—are much more important elements of future youth crime volume than population levels—which can be predicted. With large differences in rates, changes in the youth population can be expected to play a relatively minor independent role in determining the volume of youth violence. Chapter 4 shows that over the 15 years between 1995 and 2010, the youth population is expected to increase a total of 19 percent. But a large single-year increase or decrease in youth arrests will be as powerful an influence on volume as fifteen years' worth of population changes.

All of the statistical features just discussed warn us that long-range predictions about the volume of youth violence are error-prone. Offense rates are far less predictable than the size of the youth population but also much more important in determining the volume of serious violence. Assuming that any trend will continue for long is foolhardy, given the cyclical nature of youth violence. There is at least as much difference between trends in the different violent offenses as there is similarity, so that projections of trends in a single aggregation of youth violence is demonstrably erroneous.

Those reviewing figure 3.1 may notice that the increases just discussed are smaller than data reported in other studies (see, e.g., Blumstein 1995; Fox 1996; Blumstein 1995; Snyder and Sickmund 1995). The reason for the discrepancy is that many analysts use the very lowest points in juvenile violence, 1984 or 1985, as their base year. Picking a low period in a cyclically fluctuating time series will generate the greatest difference between baseline rates and current rates of violence, but it also risks confusing the up-and-down movements in a cyclical pattern with trends that represent changes in the average volume of violence to be expected over time.

What figure 3.1 shows is that rape and robbery arrests have varied substantially over the period since 1980, but there is no evidence of an underlying trend—either up or down—in the incidence of arrests over the sixteen years. This removes these two offenses from further consideration in exploring the central concern of this chapter—the assessment and explanation of trends over time. Since there is no trend, there is no reason to project any trend forward.

Homicide rates in 1996 are one-third higher than in 1980. Despite the cyclical fluctuations throughout the period, this seems sufficient ground to investigate whether a change in rate has occurred and, if so, its likely explanation. This is the task of the next section. Aggravated assault levels, which increased by more than half over the period 1980–1996, are the subject of the third section. As the following two sections show, the trends in homicide and assault are quite different in origin and policy significance.

Patterns of Youth Homicide

Figure 3.2 shows trends in homicide arrest rates for offenders 13 to 17 and over 18 over the two decades from 1976 to 1995. The two arrest rates move together first up and then down in the first decade, but then the under-18 rate takes off from 1985–1993 in a pattern that diverges from the homicide arrests in the stable, older age group.

The most important reason for the sharp escalation in homicide was an escalating volume of fatal attacks with firearms, as shown in figure 3.3. The top line is the rate of homicides by all means tied to the arrest of at least one offender under 18. The bottom line is the rate of arrests for homicides committed with all weapons other than guns, including knives, blunt objects, and personal force. The most important characteristic of the bottom line is flatness. There are minor fluctuations and no trend over time.

The middle line shows trends in arrests for homicides committed with guns, with each death that resulted in one or more arrests counted only once. Almost all of the variance during the years of the increase in total homicides was in gun cases, as was the decrease in total homicides in the early 1980s. The origins of this pattern are a puzzle. The proportion of homicides committed with guns did not increase among adults, so no general increase in handgun availability seems to explain the sharp increase in youth shootings (Zimring 1996).

That homicide increases are only gun cases has two important implications. First, it would require only a small number of attacks to change the death statistics during the 1985–1992 period. Because gunshot wounds are deadly, a relatively small number of woundings can produce a relatively large number of killings. My early studies in Chicago found a ratio of nonfatal gunshot wounds to fatalities of about seven to one, in contrast to a knife ratio of about thirty-five to one (Zimring 1968, 1972). Both numbers are undercounts because many more nonfatal woundings also go undetected. But an extra 1,700 gun killings should produce only 10,000 to 15,000 extra gun-wound cases in the aggravated assault statistics, a small percentage of the total under-18 volume.

Figure 3.2. Trends in Arrest Rates for Homicide, 1976–1996. Source: U.S. Department of Justice, Federal Bureau of Investigation (1976–1993, 1994a, 1995–1996).

Because the homicide patterns suggest that only gun assaults increased after 1985 (there were no additional nongun killings), the number of additional assault cases one would expect would be minimal, less than a 10 percent increase in all aggravated assaults, and all of these would be gun cases. But that is not what happened. The number of aggravated assault cases grew faster even than homicides after 1985. The fact that only gun homicides increased transforms the large increase in under-18 aggravated assaults into a mystery. If the increase in homicides had been distributed across all weapons, we would have expected an increase in assaults as large as the increase in homicides.

The second implication of the guns-only pattern is that the hardware used in many attacks seems to be the major explanation for the expanding rate rather than any basic change in the youth population involved in the assaults.

Every time there is an increase in youth violence, there is worry that a new, more vicious type of juvenile offender is the cause. The guns-only pattern of figure 3.3 is quite strong circumstantial evidence against the proposition that a violent new breed is a general phenomenon for three reasons. First, the sharp increase in gun use provides a clear alternative explanation for the higher number of killings by youths. It has long been thought that greater use of firearms in attacks can increase the death rate from violence independent of variations in intent because guns are more dangerous. This so-called instrumentality effect would explain a substantial increase in homicide without resort to changes in the motivations or scruples of young offenders if they are willing to use guns in attacks (Cook 1991). The second reason the gun-only pattern does not support a theory of a violent new breed of offender is that so few young attackers are involved in the switch to guns. At most, the shooters are

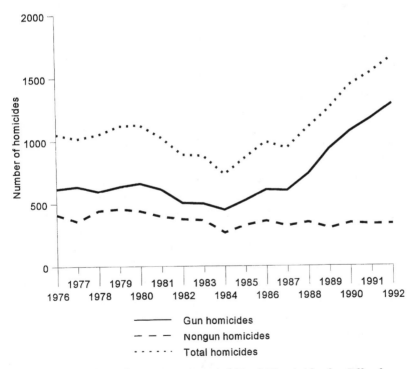

Figure 3.3. Number of Gun, Nongun, and Total Homicides by Offenders, Ages 10–17, 1976–1992. Source: U.S. Department of Justice, Federal Bureau of Investigation (1994b).

20,000 or so of the under-18 population arrested for violence. If there is a "new breed" of offender, it would have to be found only among that narrow band of firearms wounders. Third, the great majority of assaults has stayed the same over the past two decades. Knives are universally available, and the next most deadly weapon to firearms. Yet the rate of killings with knives remained stable over the eight-year expansion in total homicides. If more destructive intentions were the major cause of rate changes in homicide, some of the increase in the death rate should be found in the category of knives and other cutting instruments.

The Growth of Assault Arrests

The task here is to restate and explore the mystery in the previous discussion. Because the growth of homicides was restricted to gun cases, there is no reason to expect a large increase in the volume of aggravated assault cases over the years when homicides increased. If all forms of homicide double, one expects all forms of aggravated assault to double as well. If only gun homicides double, only aggravated assaults with guns should double, and the total serious assault rate should increase by less than 20 percent. Instead, the aggravated assault rate nearly doubled at its peak rate in 1994 and then declined at a slower pace than homicide. Is this evidence that a broad cross section of adolescents was engaging in many types of serious assaults, not limited to the gun cases? If so, why was there no increase in homicides by other means?

From a policy and planning perspective, sorting out the meaning of the expansion in aggravated assault arrests is quite important. If only homicides have increased, the number of cases is quite small. A 20 percent increase in aggravated assaults for gun assault cases is still less than a quarter of the total case increase that occurs if the true rate of youth assault doubled to a peak and fell back only 22 percent from that peak. So if the growth in aggravated assault arrests reflects the magnitude of the true growth in the volume of serious adolescent violence, the problem is much broader than an analysis of the homicide statistics would suggest.

There have been indications for some time that observers should be cautious in taking evidence about trends in youth violence from fluctuations in aggravated assault arrest levels. Twenty years ago, I was tempted to label a section on trends in police arrests for this offense "the aggravations of aggravated assault" because increases in arrest rates for this offense did not always occur when homicide rates were increasing (Zimring 1979). How assaults are counted and classified is essentially a matter of police discretion. Changing police standards can have a huge impact on statistical trends. For the period since 1980, there is significant circumstantial evidence from many sources that changing police thresholds for when assault should be recorded and when the report should be for aggravated assault are the reason for most of the growth in arrest rates.

The first evidence that reclassification is a major factor comes from arrest rates for adults. It turns out that trends over time in assault arrests for older offenders have been strikingly similar to those noted for younger offenders. But the older group experienced declines in homicide arrests over the period, so it does not seem likely that this age group is increasing in its true rate of life-threatening violence.

Figure 3.4 shows rates of aggravated assault arrests by year from 1980 to 1995 for 13- to 17-year-olds and for those 25 to 34. The 25-to-34 age group is the youngest population group that did not have any increase in homicides. (The age group 18 to 24 had trends quite similar to the 13-to-17 group. See Cook and Laub 1998.) The trends in aggravated assault arrests for the two groups are quite similar over the whole period. There are fifteen year-to-year transitions over the period, and the two groups increased together or decreased together in thirteen. Thus an upward or downward movement in the rate for one age group predicts a move in the same direction for the other age group about 85 percent of the time. The two groups behaved over time like two peas in the same statistical pod. The similar magnitude of the year-to-year changes visible in figure 3.4 is consistent with changing policy standards.

But is this evidence that trends in true rates of violence were quite similar for the two age groups, or is this evidence instead that changing police practices had the same impact on the two age groups at the same time? Homicide trends for the two age groups point toward the latter interpretation. The parallel trends for the two age groups does not hold for homicide arrests over time. Homicide arrests were sharply up for the younger group but down for the 25- to 34-year-olds, as shown in figure 3.5

Homicide arrests for the 25-to-34 age group dropped substantially after 1981 and continued a sustained decline throughout the period. There is thus no evidence that the increasing rate of serious assaults

Figure 3.4. Trends in Arrest Rates for Aggravated Assault, 1980–1995. Source: U.S. Department of Justice, Federal Bureau of Investigation (1980–1993, 1994a, 1995).

for this age group spilled over to create more deaths from assault. This suggests that the fluctuations in the older age group could not affect the volume of life-threatening assaults. The similarity of patterns over time of younger and older offenders, then, would suggest that the major reason for movements in the 13-to-17 age group should be the same as for the older group. If so, the major reason for increasing arrest rates in the younger age bracket for assault was not a change in the behavior of young offenders but a change in the classification of attacks that are close to the line that separates simple from aggravated assaults.

One way to estimate the degree to which police reclassification rather than increasing violent assault drove up aggravated assault rates is to use the trends for the older group as a proxy for reclassification. Since the homicides for this group dropped, we can assume that all of the increases that occurred in both groups were due to reclassification but that increases above and beyond those of the older group were the result of real changes. By this measure, more than 85 percent of the juvenile increase would be presumptive reclassification. (The adult rate increased 67 percent from 1980 to 1995, while the juvenile rate increased 78 percent. The adult increase was 86 percent of the juvenile increase, leaving 14 percent of that increase not accounted for by presumed reclassification.)

Simple Assault

The trends in arrests for simple assault lend strong support to the theory that police standards are shifting toward recording and upgrading assaults. Figure 3.6 shows trends in arrests for the less serious Part II offense of nonaggravated assault for 13- to 17-year-olds and 18- to 34-year-olds. The pattern produced for assaults is similar

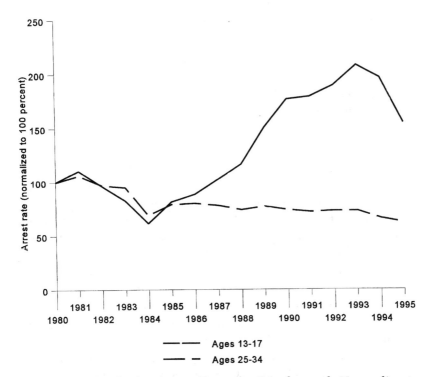

Figure 3.5. Trends in Arrest Rates for Murder and Nonnegligent Manslaughter, 1980–1995. Source: U.S. Department of Justice, Federal Bureau of Investigation (1980–1993, 1994a, 1995).

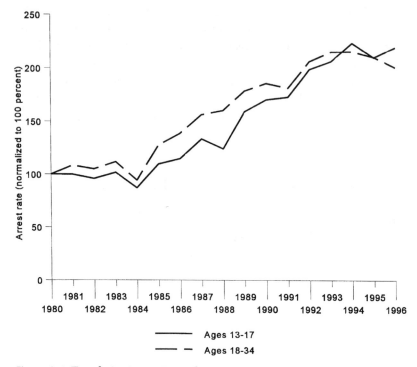

Figure 3.6. Trends in Arrest Rates for Part II Assaults, 1980–1996. Source: U.S. Department of Justice, Federal Bureau of Investigation (1980–1993, 1994a, 1995–1996).

to that observed for aggravated assaults, only more so. The growth of police recorded assault arrests is larger than for the aggravated assault category. The younger and older offenders are almost identical over time, with the two age groups moving in the same direction in thirteen of the sixteen year-to-year comparisons. The data for 1996 are an exception to this pattern, with a 10 percent increase in youth assault arrests and a 5 percent decrease for young adults. The four largest increases for the 13- to 17-year-olds occur in the same years as for the older offenders. It also turns out that three of the four largest year-to-year increases in aggravated assault match the years of the greatest increase in simple assault arrests.

The chances are substantial that a greater police willingness to report and upwardly classify assault crimes and a greater willingness to arrest those who commit assaults are contributing to the increase in arrests for both younger and older offenders. The four largest one-year increases in aggravated assault arrests amount to more than 100 percent of the total increase for aggravated assault (the four one-year jumps were 166.3 per 100,000, whereas the total increase was 160) and 83 percent of the total increase for simple assault up to 1995 (the four one-year increases were 332.4 per 100,000 of a total increase of 399.6). When all or most of the increase is concentrated in a few jumps, the likelihood that reporting thresholds are changing is higher.

Corroboration from Other Sources

A review of available data other than the Uniform Crime Reports on assault reveals three different indications that much of the change in assault statistics stems from changing police standards. The first indication is the divergent trends in assault arrests and the victimization rate reported to the National Crime Survey for assault. Figure 3.7 provides data on trends in assault arrests (combining simple and aggravated assault) and victim-reported assault for 1980–1993.

The assault arrest rate drops by 14 percent in the early 1980s, then doubles from 1985 through 1993. The reported incidence of assault victimization drops slightly in the early 1980s but then remains steady, never reaching more than 13 percent higher than the 1980 rate. The large climb in assault arrests, therefore, is not reflected in any significant change in assault victimization, a result consistent with a change in standards. Indeed, the reason that national crime survey data are not included in figure 3.7 after 1992 is also evidence of the power of changing criteria on statistics. In 1993, a new standard was used for the assault category, and the rate immediately jumped more than 80 percent. The reclassification process is not confined to police statistics.

The second piece of evidence that assaults remained more stable than official reports comes from large-scale surveys of high school boys conducted by Lloyd Johnson at the University of Michigan in 1982 and 1992. The first survey occurred at the beginning of the time series reported in figure 3.4, when aggravated assault arrests were close to the low point in the series. The second survey occurred one year short of the highest rate in the sixteen years, just short of double the official 1982 level. The survey results of involvement in serious assaults are virtually identical for the two periods. Participation in fights with injury held constant at 13 percent in the two surveys, serious fights were 17 percent in 1982 and 18 percent in 1992, and

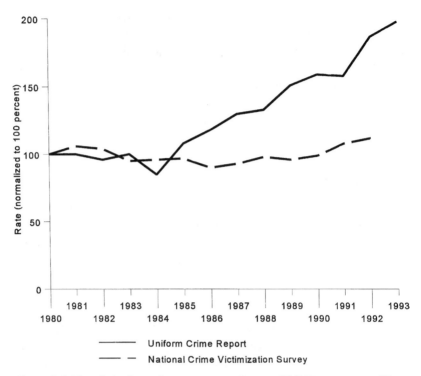

Figure 3.7. Trends in Assault, 1980–1993. Source: U.S. Department of Justice, Bureau of Justice Statistics (1980–1992); U.S. Department of Justice, Federal Bureau of Investigation (1980–1993).

weapon use was 2 percent in 1982 and 3 percent in 1992 (Bachman et al. 1984 and 1993).

The third indication of the major role of official reclassification is that the death rate for every type of assault has gone down over time. The gun assault death rate declined from 6.9 percent in 1985 to 5.6 percent in 1994. Using a case-fatality estimate technique created by Philip Cook (1991) and assuming that the additional assaults that are added were the product of reclassification without extra killings, we can see that 19 percent of the gun assaults added between 1985 and 1994 were artifactual. This case-fatality approach also estimates that 40 percent of the increase in knife assaults are probably reclassifications. For the 58 percent of aggravated assaults that involve other weapons and personal force, a declining death rate suggests that 79 percent of the additional assaults are the product of changes in police standards rather than of violent behavior. Well over half of all the additional assaults in the United States are estimated to be reclassification by this method. Because there is no detailed breakdown of aggravated assaults by age and weapon, a separate estimate only for young offenders cannot be made by using this technique.

Perspectives on Prediction

Long-range predictions about youth violence are difficult in the best of times because rates of serious offenses tend to be cyclical in unpredictable ways. But projections forward from recent trends are also problematic because there are no clear indications for the future of any violent offense to be gleaned from a careful review of current data. There are, however, important lessons about both trends and projections that should inform any discussion of what to expect in the future.

The first important finding from this analysis of recent experience is that there is no unitary trend in the recent history of youth arrests for violent crime. Homicide and assault arrests have increased, but for different reasons. Robbery and rape have fluctuated, without any discernible long-range trend. This lack of pattern has both procedural and substantive implications. The procedural lesson to be learned from the recent past is that patterns of arrest should be carefully examined one at a time rather than aggregated into a single arrest index. The substantive conclusion is that no generalization about the behavior of the current cohort of youths can be factually supported. The absence of any discernible growth trend in nonfirearms homicide, in robbery, and in rape arrest rates just does not fit generalizations about a more violent cohort, about superpredators, and the like.

Furthermore, when the two categories of growing rates are scrutinized, it turns out that youth arrests for homicides and assault have increased for different reasons. A sharp increase in gun homicide cases was the only reason the total homicide rate increased after the mid-1980s. By 1993, the rate of arrests for gun homicides had tripled from its low point, while nongun homicide was flat. Then a sharp downward trend in these arrests eliminated about half of the previous eight years of increases.

What can be applied from current information to homicide predictions is one part cliché and one part question mark. The dynamic force in the coming decade is likely to be trends in gun cases, just as it has been. But the future trend in youth gun homicide is anybody's guess. The most recent decline in gun cases has been steep, but will it be sustained? Although there is suspicion that market changes for drugs in the 1980s produced the initial increase in adolescent gun use (Blumstein 1995), speculations about why gun homicides decreased have not produced a consensus. It is difficult to predict the future course of a trend one cannot explain.

One thing is clear: There will be very little tendency for trends in homicides with guns to reflect big changes in overall rates in assault or aggravated assault. Doubling the total number of aggravated assaults with handguns would produce less than a 20 percent increase in aggravated assaults; cutting gun assaults in half would lead to a 10 percent decrease in aggravated assaults.

The largest statistical mystery of the last decade is the sharp expansion in assault and aggravated assault arrests. The same large increase occurred for the 25-to-34 age group, a group with a decline in homicide. Any reduction in the threshold between simple and aggravated assault and any shift in the minimum standard for recording an offense would have the kind of statistical impact on assault arrests that has occurred since the late 1980s. Although the matter is not beyond doubt, it appears that the willingness of police authorities to give greater priority to assaults has altered the classification of attacks across the board.

Two aspects of this possible reclassification deserve special mention. First, when this sort of reclassification occurs, there is no telling whether the old or the new threshold is the correct one. As we saw in chapter 2, the verbal description of aggravated assault is not precise, and the large number of attacks near the border between aggravated and simple assaults creates ample opportunity to justify different behavioral standards of what constitutes an aggravated assault. Second, the change in priority that motivates reclassification by the police can be very good news from a policy standpoint. More attention to particular problems often leads to reclassification of cases. Domestic violence incidents are counted as assaults more often when the problem becomes a priority. As police rejection of rape complaints (known as "unfounding") decreases, the number of rape complaints that become officially recorded incidents increases. If similar sentiments have created a higher probability that acts of violence become official statistics about violence, this is good news.

But it is good news that can be badly misinterpreted. A lower threshold for aggravating and reporting assault can produce a totally artificial crime wave in the sense that the statistics increase while the actual behavior is stable. More than half of the growth in aggravated assault by youths may be a product of this pattern during 1980–1996.

If reclassification is the principal reason for the growth in assault statistics, what further developments can be anticipated in the next decade or so? First, it is not likely that standards for arrests and for considering attacks to be aggravated assaults will revert to previous levels. There is no recurrent, cyclic pattern in crime classification over time to serve as a precedent. The larger social concern with violence that supports the efforts of the police seems to be a long-term development. Thus standards for assault arrest and for aggravated assault arrest will stay at their present levels or perhaps drop further over the coming years.

The result of these developments might well be more arrests of young persons for assault and aggravated assault. The heterogeneity of the offense category will tend to increase, and the overwhelming majority of offenses that produce arrests will be at the low end of the seriousness scale. More than ever, it will be necessary to sort out the more serious from the less serious assaults in fashioning sanctions and policy responses.

The statistical portrait of the last sixteen years is not without irony. Between 1980 and 1996, the increasing arrest rate for youth violence was concentrated in the assault category. The aggravated assault arrest rate was 41 percent of the youth violence arrest rate in 1980, yet increases in aggravated assault arrests dominated the growth over time. In 1996, the total rate of juvenile arrests for Index crimes of violence other than aggravated assault was lower than in 1980. With most of those extra aggravated assault arrests clustering at the low end of the seriousness scale, it is very likely that the average Part I arrest for an offender under 18 was for a less serious violent offense in 1996 than in 1980. It is possible that this trend will continue, so that a larger number of violence arrests will be counterbalanced by a smaller proportion at the serious end of the scale. But this kind of expansion at the shallow end of the violent crime pool is far from the growth in crime that is projected in current policy debates.

FOUR

The Case of the
Terrifying Toddlers

A remarkable part of the current dialogue about youth violence in the United States has been its future orientation. We saw in chapter 1 how the concerns and rhetoric in the mid-1990s, paralleled earlier alarms in the mid-1970s, with one significant exception. Missing from earlier eras was a focus not on current conditions but on future developments. A large number of analyses began in 1995 to project increases in the volume and severity of youth violence in the first decade of the next century. Statistical analyses of crime trends are projected to the year 2005 or 2010. Demographic data about adolescent populations have been combined with assumptions about the crime rates of future cohorts of teen offenders. For this reason, projections about the number of teenagers expected in coming years and their social characteristics are important elements in debates about policy.

One of the earlier versions of this type of warning was issued by James Q. Wilson (1995):

> Meanwhile, just beyond the horizon, there lurks a cloud that the winds will soon bring over us. The population will start getting younger again. By the end of this decade there will be a million more people between the ages of fourteen and seventeen than there are now; this increase will follow the decade of the 1980s when people in that age group declined, not only as a proportion of the total but in absolute numbers. This extra million will be half male. Six percent of them will become high rate, repeat offenders—30,000 more young muggers, killers, and thieves than we have now. Get ready. (p. 507)

One year later, John DiIulio (1996) of Princeton pushed the horizon back ten years and upped the ante: "By the year 2010, there will be approximately 270,000 more juvenile super-predators on the streets than there were in 1990" (p. 1).

James Fox (1996) of Northeastern University described the projected volume of homicide involvements in 2005 as "a blood bath." The National Center for Juvenile Courts project a doubling of juvenile arrests by 2010 (Snyder and Sickmund 1995). The Washington-based Council on Crime in America (1996) warned of "a coming storm of juvenile violence." What all of these estimates have in common is that demographic projections play a central role in predictions about the volume of youth crime. Suddenly, population statistics have become an important element in criminal justice policy planning.

This chapter considers the two types of demographic measures that have caused concern over trends in youth crime in the next fifteen years. The first section examines available data on the volume of adolescents, focusing on the age group 13 to 17. The next section addresses some of the qualitative changes in youths and the conditions under which they will go through childhood. The last section examines the deterministic logic of these projections.

Too Many Teenagers?

There are two important methods of measuring the impact of a particular population subgroup on a social environment. One is to count the number of persons in the age group, a natural way of determining its impact. Figure 4.1 provides that information for the actual and projected youth population between the ages of 13 and 17 in the United States from 1960 until 2010. Of course, the last fourteen data points are estimated, but because most of the people counted in these estimates already reside in the United States, the margin of error is small. Those 13 to 17 are the focus of this time series because they have the highest juvenile arrest statistics.

This teen population increased rapidly during the 1960s and early 1970s and then peaked in 1975 at 21 million. The fifteen years of sharp growth were followed by fifteen years of decline, with the midteen population bottoming out in 1990 at 16 million. The Census Bureau expects the number of teenagers to grow 16 percent over the fifteen years ending in 2010, to a total of 21.5 million. The growth rate for this period is projected at about 1 percent per year, slightly more than a third of the growth rate experienced during the 1960s. By 2010, the United States will have just under a half million more teenagers than were in the population in 1975. On the sheer number of teenagers, the United States will have spent thirty years breaking even.

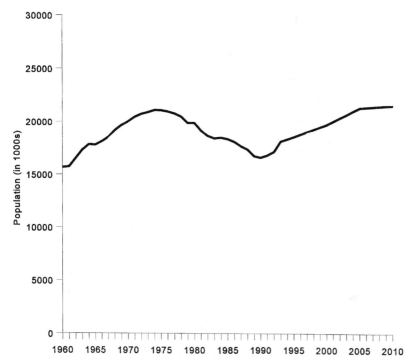

Figure 4.1. Trends in Youth Population, Ages 13–17, 1960–2010. Source: U.S. Department of Commerce, Bureau of the Census (1960–1994, 1995a).

The simple counting of a teenaged population in the style of figure 4.1 is poor demography in one important respect—it provides no information about the social setting of the United States in the various years for which there are population estimates. Figure 4.2 is an easy if partial cure for this condition by reporting the proportion of the total U.S. population between the ages of 13 and 17 for the half-century beginning in 1960. It provides an important context for the growth of the youth population in the 1960s and early 1970s, a period when the teenage population was expanding far more quickly than the population as a whole. At its 1975 peak, the 13-to-17 age group was 9.9 percent of the total population, having grown twice as fast as the rest of the population. From 1975 to 1990, the proportionate share of the population in the midteens dropped even faster than it had expanded in the previous fifteen years; at 6.7 percent, the older juvenile share of the U.S. population had dropped 3.2 percent.

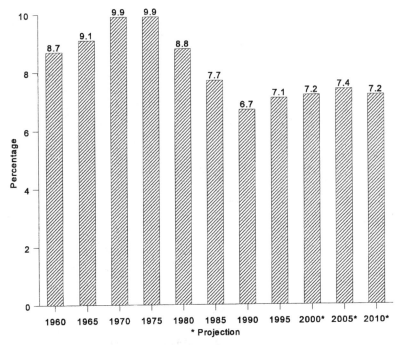

Figure 4.2. Proportion of U.S. Population, Ages 13–17, 1960–2010. Source: U.S. Department of Commerce, Bureau of the Census (1960–1994, 1995a).

Thus projected increases in the youth population might look large from a 1990 base because the proportion of youths in the U.S. population was at its low point for a generation.

The most important lesson from figure 4.2 concerns the impact of expanding numbers of youths on the population as a whole. From 1990 to 2010, the share of the population in the 13-to-17 age group will expand from 6.7 percent to 7.2 percent. This increase will take the midteen proportion one-sixth of the way back to the youth share of 1975, recapturing 0.5 percent of the 3.2 percent loss generated from 1975 to 1990. The 7.2 percent share expected for 2010 is significantly less than the 8.7 share noted for 1960, before the huge growth associated with the crime-prone 1960s.

This relatively low concentration of middle teenagers occurs even when the number of youths expands to a record high for a simple reason—the growth of the U.S. population. The 21 million youths in the United States in 1975 lived in a nation of 213 million. The 21 million-plus youths in 2010 will live among a U.S. population of 300 million.

In this context, it does not seem that the age structure of the U.S. population in the coming years should be of particular concern. The modest expansion of the adolescent share of the total population will be neither abrupt nor extreme. There will be no large bulge in the young end of the age scale, challenging with sheer numbers the institutions that socialize youths. The increased burden on schools and youth-serving institutions will be more than offset in due course by a modest expansion in the working-age population needed to support the retirement years of baby boomers. Why all the fuss?

Fighting the Last War?

Once the demographic data on the age structure of the U.S. population are placed in long-range context, it is difficult to comprehend why the expansion of the youth population is perceived as a particular problem. However, even the modest expansions just outlined have produced concern among commentators for three reasons.

The first concern is the arithmetic of the interaction of the expanding population with high or increasing rates of arrest. If rates of serious violence do go up, a 16 percent expansion in the youth population would make a bad situation somewhat worse (see Fox 1996). There is no flaw in the arithmetic of this type of projection, but putting the emphasis on the small increase in population rather than on the high crime rates that such projections assume is incorrect. If juvenile homicide rates double, the situation would be troublesome even if the volume of teenagers were to decline 5 percent. Population trends are not the real problem.

A second concern comes from memories of the 1960s, when the explosive growth of the youth population was one of many simultaneous criminogenic changes in the American urban landscape. Wilson, who was the first to sound an alarm in the 1990s about a million extra teenagers, had earlier written about the huge impact of demography in the 1960s:

> Well before the war in Vietnam had fully engaged us or the ghetto riots had absorbed us, the social bonds—the ties of family, of neighborhood, of mutual forbearance and civility— seem to have come asunder. Why?
> That question should be, and no doubt in time will be, seri-

ously debated. No single explanation, perhaps no set of explanations, will ever gain favor. One fact, however, is an obvious beginning to an explanation: by 1962 and 1963 there had come of age the persons born during the baby boom of the immediate postwar period. A child born in 1946 would have been sixteen in 1962, seventeen in 1963.

The numbers involved were very large. In 1950 there were about 24 million persons aged fourteen to twenty-four; by 1960 that had increased only slightly to just under 27 million. But during the next ten years it increased by over 13 million persons. Every year for ten years, the number of young people increased by 1.3 million. That ten-year increase was greater than the growth in the young segment of the population for the rest of the *century* put together. To state it in another way that focuses on the critical years of 1962 and 1963, during the first *two* years of the decade of the 1960s, we added more young persons (about 2.6 million) to our population than we had added in any preceding *ten* years since 1930.

The result of this has been provocatively stated by Professor Norman B. Ryder, the Princeton University demographer: "There is a perennial invasion of barbarians who must somehow be civilized and turned into contributors to fulfillment of the various functions requisite to societal survival." That "invasion" is the coming of age of a new generation of young people. Every society copes with this enormous socialization process more or less successfully, but occasionally that process is almost literally swamped by a quantitative discontinuity in the numbers of persons involved: "The increase in the magnitude of the socialization tasks in the United States during the past decade was completely outside the bounds of previous experience."

If we continue Professor Ryder's metaphor, we note that in 1950 and still in 1960 the "invading army" (those aged fourteen to twenty-four) were outnumbered three to one by the size of the "defending army" (those aged twenty-five to sixty-four). By 1970 the ranks of the former had grown so fast that they were only outnumbered two to one by the latter, a state of affairs that had not existed since 1910. (J. Q. Wilson 1974:12–13)

The experience in the 1960s may well have alerted observers to the potential role of population changes. But why the alarm over very modest growth in the period 1990–2010? Two clichés compete to provide an explanation. The first is "once bitten, twice shy," suggesting a reluctance on the part of policy analysts to let another population-led crime wave sneak up on them. But the second cliché, the complaint that too many strategists seem always to be fighting the last war, seems closer to the truth. The coming of age of the baby boomers in the 1960s is in no important sense a precedent for the demographic shifts expected in the next fifteen years.

Some Qualitative Concerns

A third reason is offered in current analyses for worry about the growth in youth populations—the theory that a large proportion of current and future teens will be at risk of high rates of crime and social disadvantage. This type of concern is based not just on the number of young persons in the population but also on their social characteristics. Because a large proportion of tomorrow's children and youths may be at special risk, it can be argued that increases in the teen population that might ordinarily not cause trouble should now be regarded with alarm. Whether the focus of concern is poverty, single-parent households, educational gaps, or ethnicity and color, this is a concern about changes in the composition of the nation's population rather than about numbers.

Many important characteristics of the youth population of 2010 cannot be predicted with confidence long in advance. Among these are youth poverty and educational status and attainment. But the racial and ethnic composition of 1997's 2-year-olds is a pretty good indication of the racial and ethnic profile of 15-year-olds in 2010, and expected changes in the racial and ethnic mix of the youth population have played an important role in the concerns of many people about "the coming storm" of juvenile crime. The data in figure 4.3 show the changing mix in the proportion of 13- to 17-year-olds classified African American, Hispanic, and all others.

The growth pattern is quite different for the African-American and Hispanic segments of the youth population. The former's share of total adolescent population aged 13 to 17 increased from 13.2 percent in 1970 to 15.5 percent in 1987, an increase of 2.3 percent in seventeen years. In the twenty-three years after 1987, it is projected that the African-American share of the youth population will grow less than a point, from 15.5 percent to 16.4 percent. The number of African-American teens will grow substantially, but three-quarters of the increase will be just keeping pace with the growth of the total youth population.

The Hispanic teen population, in contrast, is in the middle of a

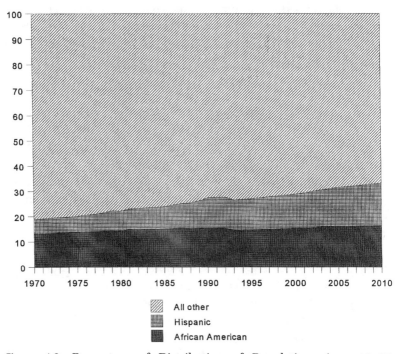

Figure 4.3. Percentage of Distribution of Population, Ages 13–17, 1970–2010. Source: U.S. Department of Commerce, Bureau of the Census (1995a).

growth pattern much larger than that of the rest of the youth population. In 1970, there were 1.14 million Hispanic-surname youths between the ages of 13 and 17 in the United States, according to the Census Bureau's estimate, or 5.7 percent of the population in that age group. By 2010, the number of Hispanic teens is estimated to be 3.63 million, and the Hispanic share of the 13-to-17 age group is expected to have tripled, to 16.9 percent.

The theory that the racial and ethnic composition of the youth population should influence the rate of youth violence is straightforward but untested. It is thought that since particular segments of the population have higher than average risks at any one time, the larger the share of that high-risk group in a future population, the higher the rate of violence we can expect in the future.

Thus, since African-American youths are currently arrested for homicide at a rate much higher than youths from other backgrounds, one of two quite different conclusions might arise:

1. An increase in the African-American percentage of a future youth population can be noted as a feature of the future youth population that might tend to push rates of total youth violence somewhat higher than they might otherwise be.
2. A total youth homicide rate for some future date could be projected by multiplying this year's rate of African-American homicide arrests by 2010's expected volume of African-American teens, then multiplying this year's rate of white teen homicide arrests times 2010's expected volume of white teens, and adding the totals together to estimate total homicide arrests. (A separate calculation for Hispanics would also be possible in this pattern, except that reliable data are not available.)

The first tactic is, I believe, justified, as long as the considerable limits of using population characteristics to project rates of behavior are acknowledged (Zimring 1975). The second approach is doomed to catastrophic error. It is unjustified precisely because race, ethnicity, gender, and other social factors are not the determining characteristics of the rate of lethal violence in a population over time.

Rates of serious violence are much higher in big cities than in towns and suburbs, among males than among females, and among African Americans than among Caucasians. What this means is that, all other things being equal, a larger concentration of a future population in the higher-risk category will be associated with a higher rate of serious violence than will a future population with fewer males, fewer city dwellers, and fewer blacks. The problem with assuming that last year's rate of arrests for African-American males will hold steady for the next two decades is that "all other things" are rarely equal for two years, let alone twenty years. Figure 4.4 shows the fluctuations in male arrest rates for homicide over the period 1980–1995.

What the gyrations in figure 4.4 show is how many other influences over time have a substantial impact on the particular rates at which risk groups are arrested and presumably also are committing offenses. The early 1980s are a sobering case in point. The African-American share of the youth population went up by seven-tenths of a point in four years, and the homicide arrest rate of males in the age group dropped 38 percent. In contrast, the African-American share of the total youth population was stable from 1985 to 1993, whereas the youth homicide rate was climbing by unprecedented lengths. Fluctuations in the percentage of the youth population that is black do not track movements upward or downward in the youth homicide arrest

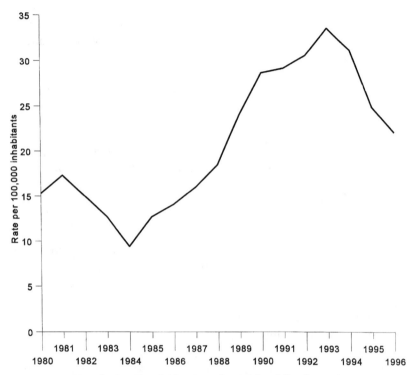

Figure 4.4. Trends in Homicide Rate for Male Offenders, Ages 13–17, 1980–1996. Source: U.S. Department of Justice, Federal Bureau of Investigation (1980–1993, 1994a, 1995–1996).

rates over the past twenty years very well because they play a very minor role in determining arrest rates for serious crimes of violence; also, the changing social environment of youths has had such a substantial impact on these rates in relatively short periods of time.

To project any single year's aggregate arrest rates forward for fifteen years seems unjustified as a projection technique, as discussed in chapter 3. The lowest homicide rate in the last seventeen years is less than one-third of the highest (5.3 versus 17.9). The most recent rate is 11.4, almost at the midpoint between these extremes. Which rate should we use for a projection?

The high margin for error in projections can be illustrated from very recent history. James Fox (1996) of Northeastern University produced a series of projected rates for 1994 through 2010. Two projections were provided—a lower series, which assumed that all future years would experience youth homicide arrests at 1993 rates, and a higher series, which assumed a continual growth in homicide arrest rates. His estimates were obsolete before the ink was dry on the report. The projected lower estimate is 33 percent higher than the actual homicide total for 1996; the higher estimate is more than 40 percent higher. The reason for these gross short-term errors is clear. The variations in the homicide rate in two years—1995 and 1996—were much more important than the growth of the youth population would be for fifteen years in determining the volume of homicide arrests. Since the future homicide rate is a guess, so, too, is the projection of future homicide volume.

There are three further points to be made about qualitatively informed projections of future homicides by teens, even though none is as important as the fundamental imponderables that preclude predicting future homicide rates. First, one significant risk characteristic for criminal homicide is diminishing over time in the United States—presence in a large central city. The homicide rate inside the city limits of the twenty largest cities in the United States was four times as high as in the rest of the nation (Zimring and Hawkins 1997:65), and youth homicides were even more intensely concentrated in major cities in the early 1990s (see Blumstein and Rosenfeld 1998). The long-established trend is toward a smaller proportion of the youth population to be found in major cities. Over the twenty years between 1970 and 1990, the proportion of all U.S. youths aged 10 to 17 who lived inside the ten largest cities dropped from 9.29 percent to 8.34 percent (U.S. Department of Commerce, Bureau of the Census 1970, 1990). Although this may seem like a small drop, the 10.2 percent reduction in the proportion of all youths in the highest risk environment means that the total youth population could expand by 10 percent without *any* more youths living in the highest risk areas. This dispersion of the population away from large central cities should reduce youth homicide rates if everything else holds constant.

But this shrinkage in the big-city share of the youth population was overwhelmed after 1985 by the soaring rates among those teens who remained in big cities. So the good news about population dispersion must be tempered by the same inability to predict homicide rates from risk factors that we observe when tracing the impact of changes in race and ethnicity.

Second, the subset of the population with the largest change—Hispanic origin or surname—is not a population group in which homicide offense propensities can be determined reliably from available sources, let alone projected into the future. What makes a 14-year-old an "Hispanic"? His last name? The national origin of one of his parents? There is no database on homicide from which good estimates of arrest or offense rates can be projected for this group in any single year, let alone over time. There is thus very little improvement in projections that disaggregate minority populations because the major changes in the population will involve a population group without any reliably documented risk propensities.

Third, none of the factors of concern about family structure—illegitimacy, single-parent status, and so on—can be used to inform homicide projections because none of these characteristics has any known link to the expected volume of adolescent homicide in the United States or anywhere else. (This matter is addressed in detail in chapter 10.) Without any data on social risk factors, the "qualitatively informed" projections of future homicide volume are, in reality, matters of accounting for gender and ethnicity.

Still, is it not better to make these estimates with detailed data about race and ethnicity than without such data? Not necessarily. If the race-specific projections of homicide volume are going to overestimate the actual volume, as every one of them would do for 1995 and 1996, omitting the racial and ethnic details will actually reduce the level of error. More details in projections can just as easily compound a statistical error as reduce it.

I do not mean to suggest that the circumstances of the youth population in the next fifteen years are irrelevant to the life opportunities or criminal behavior of the teenagers of 2010. But projecting levels of an infrequent and variable behavior like juvenile homicide from estimates of a youth population in future years is foolhardy. It is not that we do not know enough about the causes of youth homicide to make reliable estimates of future homicides. Quite the opposite. We know too much about the variability of homicide to engage in such numerological guessing games in the name of science.

Determinism without Portfolio

The social scientific evidence for the current argument that a fixed percentage of a population of males will constitute a predatory menace in the year 2010 is a classic case study of compounded distortion. The story begins with a finding by Marvin Wolfgang, Robert

Figlio, and Thorsten Sellin (1972) that about 6 percent of Philadelphia boys would accumulate five or more police contacts before their eighteenth birthday. This was first noted with respect to a large group of boys born in Philadelphia in 1945, who turned 18 in 1963. Rates of violent crime were relatively low in those days, even in Philadelphia, but whatever violent crime was found in the cohort was concentrated among the most arrested 6 percent of the male population. The correct label for this group of juveniles is chronic delinquents. Many had some form of violent crime in their police records; many did not.

Many other studies in other settings and in other periods have found that a high proportion of whatever delinquencies are found in a large group of boys will be concentrated in the most active delinquents. In Philadelphia, where there is a good deal of life-threatening violence, the rate of violence in the most active 6 percent of delinquents will be fairly high. In Racine, Wisconsin, the rate of serious violence even among the most active boys will be much lower (compare Wolfgang et al. 1972 with Shannon et al. 1991). The fact that offenses tend to concentrate in small subsegments of a juvenile population does not predict what forms of offenses will be found in the subsample or how many acts of life-threatening violence will occur. The finding of concentration thus has no validity in predicting the particular components of juvenile crime.

The concentration of delinquency is the foundation of James Q. Wilson's (1995:507) prediction of "30,000 more muggers, killers and thieves than we have now." Wilson gets the 30,000 figure by estimating 6 percent of 500,000 extra adolescent males. This formulation has a substantial capacity to mislead. The three types of criminals are listed in a way that invites the reader to conclude that muggers and killers will be as numerous as thieves. This recalls the classic English recipe for horse and hare stew: "equal parts horse and hare: one horse, one hare." The reader is further invited to assume that the expansion in the youth population is the dynamic that will generate a larger volume of killing and robbing in the juvenile population: "Get ready!"

The next stop toward the prediction of a "coming storm of juvenile violence" is DiIulio's exponential exaggeration of James Q. Wilson's prediction. Whereas Wilson (1995) speaks of 6 percent of juvenile males as "muggers, killers and thieves," DiIulio (1995) coins the phrase "super-predator." Thus we have had a category of young children years away from adolescence transformed from future "chronic delinquents" to prospective "muggers, killers and thieves" to tomorrow's "juvenile super-predators" on sheer rhetorical horsepower. And suddenly, Wilson's 30,000 has become an army of "approximately 270,000 more super-predators." Why does DiIulio estimate an increment eight times as great as Wilson's?

A detailed answer to that question tells us much about the lack of scrutiny of data in the policy debate about juvenile justice in the United States today. Both James Q. Wilson and DiIulio estimate an additional population of hard-core juvenile offenders based on the 6 percent figure from Wolfgang et al. (1972). But Wilson (1995) concentrates on the 1990–2000 period, which makes a small difference in his estimate and restricts it to youths who will be old enough to be committing offenses by the year 2000. DiIulio (1995) arrives at the figure of 270,000 extra superpredators by noting that the number of boys under 18 in the United States is expected to grow from 32 million to 36.5 million from 1996 to 2010. By assuming that serious delinquents will be 6 percent of that population, he arrives at the number 270,000 (.06 × 4.5 million = 270,000).

One clue that something is wrong here is that this arithmetic would suggest that there are already 1.9 million juvenile superpredators on U.S. streets (32 million current boys × 0.06 = 1,920,000). That happens to be more young people than were accused of any form of delinquency last year in the United States. The special error here is that DiIulio (1996) assumes that not merely 6 percent of teenagers but also 6 percent of all youths are superpredators. In 2010, fewer than 30 percent of the population under 18 will be 13 years of age and over in the extra cohort and just as many 5 years of age and younger. Since 93 percent of all juvenile crime is committed by youths aged 13 and older, fewer than a third of the "extra 270,000" will be active at all in 2010. But the rest, argues DiIulio, will be waiting in the wings, coming at us "in waves." Thus we are to believe that the youths born in 2009 are just as surely superpredators-in-waiting as the 10-year-olds who are behind in reading or the 14-year-olds with a first arrest for petty theft or drug use. We may not know who they are, but we know that they are there because 6 percent of a male population will meet the criterion.

There are three things to say about this reductio ad absurdum. First, even though the numbers involved in this exercise are rather extreme, the predictions and terminology were not seriously challenged for many months after the analysis first appeared in February 1996. That July, the Republican candidate for president made a radio speech on juvenile crime, using the term "superpredator," and informed his listeners that the juvenile arrest rate would double by 2010 (see Zimring 1996). Even extreme claims survive easily in an environment that lacks quality controls for forecasting techniques.

Second, the saga of juvenile superpredators has enormous political benefits. To talk of a "coming storm" creates a riskless environment for getting tough in advance of the future threat. If the crime rate rises, the prediction has been validated. If the crime rate does not rise, the policies that the alarmists put in place can be credited with avoiding the bloodbath. The prediction cannot be falsified, currently or ever.

Third, the wild arithmetic and colorful language of the DiIulio (1995) scenario should not distract observers from the central fallacy of his prediction, a fallacy that animates the James Q. Wilson (1995) work as well. The only proper inference to be drawn from knowing that an extra million teenagers will be present at some future time is that there will be a larger group of teenagers. If delinquency is concentrated in 6 percent of the male population, an increase in the youth population will also increase the number in that 6 percent. How many muggers or killers will be in that population is not known or predicted by the concentration finding.

Thus, even if their adjectives were carefully chosen and their numbers were realistic, the prediction technique used by James Q. Wilson (1995) and John DiIulio (1995) is empty of logical or empirical content. If the argument implied is that the number of homicides or robberies generated by a youth cohort can be easily predicted by its relative size, this is far from obvious in the record of recent American history. The rate of youth violence increased in the late 1980s even as the youth population declined, and the volume of youth violence decreased after 1993 as the youth population grew.

But a deeper point must be made. The reason we cannot currently estimate the volume of juvenile homicide in the United States in 2010 is not merely that we lack an appropriate technology or sufficiently fancy social science. Prediction is beyond our capacity because the conditions that will influence the homicide rates among children now 4 years old when they turn 17 have not yet been determined. The incidence of homicide and other forms of life-threatening violence varies widely over time and is not susceptible to good long-range actuarial estimates even for large groups. It is not possible to know about the homicide rate in 2010 because so many of its key determinants are part of an American history that has yet to happen. Will the schools get better or worse? What patterns of juvenile handgun availability and use will we experience toward the end of the first decade of the twenty-first century? What levels of street drug traffic will urban areas have and with what resultant lethal violence? Most of what will determine the homicide rate among today's 4-year-olds has not yet occurred.

A Manifesto for Disinvestment

To imagine otherwise is to live in a world where a label like "violent delinquent" becomes a hereditary title, an inverse earldom of the urban ghetto. That pattern of thought has two troublesome consequences. To adopt a hard determinist account of lethal violence fifteen years down the road makes efforts at improving the environments that influence violence seem far less urgent. If school does not divert youths from hard-core juvenile violence, why care about educational improvements? If future violence is preordained, why waste efforts and resources in trying to stop it? A fatalistic determinism can be an excuse for disinvestment in urban youth development.

Blaming the Toddler

Another latent function of deterministic accounts of criminal violence is rather peculiar. If we really believed that the shape of serious criminal careers were determined early in childhood, future predators would not deserve unqualified blame. After all, the ruthless forces that shaped their careers were much more powerful than their personalities.

But just the opposite view seems to lie in the rush to identify tomorrow's superpredators before their diapers are dry. In the current juvenile justice debate, it often seems that people use descriptions of future criminality as a device to look past the current dependency and tender years of children, to blame them in advance for the terrible crimes we imagine they will someday commit. This type of projection is certainly not morally coherent, but fear and resentment have never been effective teachers of moral principle.

Conclusion

There will be a middle-sized increase in the youth population over the period 1995–2010, but the percentage of the population in the crime-prone ages of 13 to 17 will be much lower than in the mid-

1970s. The percentage of the youth population that is African American will increase by less than 1 percent over the period 1987–2010, whereas the percentage of the youth population that is Hispanic will increase substantially.

The impact of all these changes in the number and composition of the youth population on rates of serious violence is not known. A 19 percent increase in the population will have a modest impact on crime volume. If the rate of serious violence goes down at the rate of the early 1980s or mid-1990s, a 19 percent population increase will not dilute the decline of crime dividend by much. If the rate of serious violence increases substantially, the additional population will make the problem somewhat worse. But population will not be the big story in violent youth crime in the foreseeable American future, and concern about crime should not be a major issue in planning for changes in the youth population.

Part II

LEGAL POLICY TOWARD
YOUTH VIOLENCE

Basic principles and careful analysis would be necessary in the construction of rational legal policies toward youth violence in any era. In the present circumstances of public alarm and legislative haste, principles and analyses are an urgent necessity. This part of the book addresses the general framework of principles required to construct policies toward youth violence and then pursues three key issues that require sustained analysis in the current circumstances.

Chapter 5 discusses the basic principles that should animate the legal responses to adolescent violence. Why are adolescents who commit violent acts different from violent adults? Why are they different from nonviolent adolescents? The discussion in this chapter is a necessary background to the analyses in chapters 6, 7, and 8.

Chapter 6 examines the peculiar and important issue of firearms policies. Scrutiny of recent trends in youth violence revealed that the increased use of firearms in assaults was the most significant explanation for the increase in homicides. Keeping handguns from the young is an island of consensus in the otherwise bitterly divisive debate about gun control in the United States, but chapter 6 also demonstrates how the widespread availability of firearms complicates the task of making the teen years a gun free period of American life. Prohibiting youthful gun ownership may be a popular goal, but achieving it is a costly and complicated task.

Chapter 7 discusses the criteria that govern whether juveniles accused of serious violent offenses should be transferred to the jurisdiction of the criminal courts. Changes in these standards have been the most common legislative response to public concern about youth violence. But recent legislation has not been governed by principled debate, and chapter 7 tries to fill this gap.

Chapter 8 confronts the hardest of the hard cases in legal policy, the legal response to adolescents who take human life. These are the cases that scare and confuse us. Is the immaturity of an offender relevant to deserved punishment when his or her actions have caused a death? How can the need for retribution and public protection be balanced against the requirements of penal proportionality in homicide cases? There is surprisingly little legal scholarship on this particular problem. Yet a jurisprudence of youth violence without principles for homicide cases is like a house without a roof. Chapter 8 is my attempt to address the multiplicity of issues that must be resolved to build a coherent legal policy for adolescent homicides.

FIVE

Some Basic Principles

The chapter addresses the basic principles that should govern a wide range of harmful acts that occur in an age range from about 12 to 20. This is a very broad spectrum of policy and behavior, so these remarks cannot be considered comprehensive coverage. Instead, what is offered is usually called "notes toward" in the academic tradition, by which the author implies that a complete jurisprudence is his or her next project (but one, of course, that never seems to get written). The general discussion in this chapter is preliminary to the specific questions considered in chapters 6, 7, and 8.

My version of "notes toward" comes in four installments. The first discusses the substitution of debates about procedure and court jurisdiction for issues of substantive principle. The second discusses the policy for youth violence as an extension of the legal policy for crime, as well as an extension of policy for youth development. The question is not which of these two perspectives should control thinking about youth violence but how they can jointly determine appropriate responses to particular circumstances. The third part is the heart of this chapter, in which an attempt is made to identify two clusters of policies in more detail than in previous efforts (Zimring 1978). The fourth part considers whether special dispensations for youths should not also be extended to violent youths. The aim of the chapter is to provide a framework to inform the large number of specific questions that a useful policy must address one by one.

Substance Versus Procedure

Juvenile violence raises issues for the justice system that involve both the substance and the procedures that it uses to respond to particular acts. The substantive issues are whether punishment is appropriate for particular acts, the degree to which youths and the conditions associated with youth should affect the appropriate punishment in individual cases, and the purposes of punishment that should de-

termine the response to violent acts of varying degrees of seriousness. The procedural issues are whether a particular young person
should be referred to a juvenile or a criminal court and what procedural provisions should govern the hearing of particular cases.

To some extent, the choice of court—juvenile or criminal—might
determine both the procedures and the substantive principles that
will govern a specific case, but this link is by no means a matter of
logical necessity. The same principles about responsibility and mitigation can be invoked in both juvenile and criminal courts. It is
widely assumed that these two different court systems employ very
different philosophies and standards, but such assumptions have not
been established by careful empirical study.

Thus, one troublesome feature in the debate about responses to
youth violence is the dominance of jurisdictional concerns. Almost
all the policy discussion about the treatment of young violent offenders in the legal system is about which court system should handle
particular types of cases. Political debates and academic discourse
are both jurisdictionally focused and most concerned with the procedures that will be used to assign particular cases. Substantive principles are rarely considered as policies that might apply in either juvenile or criminal courts for different kinds of cases or policies that
might be changed to accommodate different circumstances. Instead,
the implicit assumption seems to be that each of the court systems
has a single stereotyped set of priorities for dealing with all the
young offenders before it and, further, that nothing can or should be
done to alter this set of mutually antagonistic institutional biases.

Juvenile court is where, it is assumed, young offenders are sent to
be coddled, reformed, and protected. Criminal courts are assumed to
be institutions where the youthfulness of a defendant will be ignored, and only considerations about the seriousness of the offense
and the need for deterrence and incapacitation will control the outcome. If the orientation and outcome in each court are uniform and
unvaried, the only important question is which court should get
jurisdiction.

The preoccupation with which court should have jurisdiction
would make sense only if the current legal system for processing
young offenders was itself both monstrous and arbitrary—a single dividing line, separating systems with totally inconsistent principles
and no capacity to compromise in either youth protection or crime
control. The juvenile court would pursue one unvarying policy, no
matter what the offense; the criminal court would also be limited to a

single policy, and that policy would contradict the assumptions and priorities of the juvenile justice system.

Of course, the criminal courts and juvenile courts of the real world are much more complicated and much more subject to variation than in these stereotypes. Punishment and responsibility are not foreign concepts in the modern juvenile court, and diminished responsibility as a consequence of immaturity is important in the decisions reached in criminal courts. Thus there is no sense in which the proper principles for deciding any particular case can be derived from just knowing which court will hear it. The substantive principles that come into play when considering the appropriate responses are more important than the court that will have jurisdiction. Therefore, the discussion of proper substantive principles should also precede any consideration of appropriate form. Rightly considered, the institutions of justice should be servants of substantive principle. That perspective demands prior attention to substance.

The current debate, by stressing only the issue of which court prevails, is not, strictly speaking, putting the cart before the horse. There is often no horse. One reason basic principles are ignored is that they are not evident on the agenda. Thus a debate focused on jurisdiction is not merely silly; it also carries costs.

This chapter attempts to restore the primacy of substantive issues by first discussing the principles in competition when very young persons inflict serious harm on their victims.

Two Standards of Comparison

Sentencing policy for young offenders is located at the crossroad between legal policy for youth development and legal policy for criminal offenders. A 16-year-old boy shoots and wounds another youth. The question of the appropriate legal response to this act by this actor is a matter of both crime policy and youth policy. From the perspective of crime control, the question is determining the extent to which 16-year-olds who shoot and wound should be treated in the same way or differently from older persons who commit the same offense. From the perspective of youth policy, the issue is determining whether 16-year-olds who shoot and wound should be treated similarly or differently from other 16-year-olds. If policy for young offenders is properly classified as both youth policy and crime policy, these two standards should not be thought of as competitors in determining which should dominate decision making. Instead, both perspectives should jointly inform policy determination.

From a perspective of youth development, what separates the 16-year-old who shoots and wounds from others his age is the harm of his act and the moral culpability of his intention to commit an act that causes great harm. Even if youth policy were the only set of principles used to decide legal policy in this case, the harm and culpability associated with the act would justify the maximum exertion of social control available to a youth policy. One does not need a separate criminal law system to tell the difference between 16-year-olds who wound with deadly weapons and other youths. Any youth-serving institution will treat these juveniles and these acts separately.

From a criminal law perspective, what separates 16-year-olds from older persons who shoot is diminished culpability, even for intended harms, because of immaturity and because of a youth's lessened capacity and experience with self-control. Even if a criminal law perspective were the only tool available for making legal policy in this case, the youth and immaturity of a criminal actor would be relevant to the proper determination of punishment.

So the factors of importance in penal considerations and those that influence youth policy are not mutually exclusive. There are also policy perspectives that are not shared by these two systems but that should influence policy when they overlap. Youth development policy takes risks with the general public welfare to allow young persons to try out adult privileges like driving even though adolescents are especially dangerous before they are experienced drivers. We take the special risks of this learning period because there is no way to avoid them when the only effective way to learn an activity is by doing it (Zimring 1982:Chap. 7). For similar reasons, the system may wish to avoid punishments that inflict substantial permanent harm on young offenders so that a healthy transition to adulthood is still possible even when harmful mistakes are made.

But the larger dangers of adolescent privilege also produce restrictions on the way young persons can behave that are not present for adults. Activities like drinking, smoking, and purchasing handguns are not available to 17-year-olds. These special limitations of adolescent liberty are based on the same notions of immaturity that reduce the culpability of young persons for criminal acts. I show in the next section that status offenses and diminished penal responsibility are two sides of the same coin.

Techniques of Denial

There is at least some evident tension between the punitive tug of crime control policy and the protective tug of youth development policy when young persons commit serious crimes. Debates about youth crime policy have produced many rhetorical gambits that seek to avoid this tension. The crudest method of seeking to remove young offenders from the coverage of youth protective policy is to re-name them. When terms like "juvenile superpredator" and "feral presocial being" are used in debates about youth crime, they have a special rhetorical purpose. A "superpredator" is posited as some-thing very different from a youth, and the proponent of renaming thus argues that no special provisions of a youth policy need apply to any person that can be so classified (Bennett, DiIulio, and Waters 1996).

A second device tries to link the intention to commit serious criminal harms with a maturity and commitment to criminal activi-ties that is inconsistent with legal treatment as a youth. In statutes providing for waiver to criminal courts, juvenile court judges are asked to decide whether particular accused persons are mature. If they are, they can be punished as adults (see, e.g., *Kent v. United States,* 383 U.S. 541, 1966). This notion that maturity of an adoles-cent can be used to deny any obligation for special treatment was re-cently invoked by a Venezuelan official who was explaining why it was not objectionable to house juveniles in adult jails: "The Latin American minor is not the European minor. He is mentally an adult" (Schemo 1997).

The transfer of young persons below the maximum age of juvenile court jurisdiction to criminal court if they are found to be too mature or too sophisticated for the former has a history in the United States just as long as that of the juvenile court. One year before Judge Julian Mack (1909) published his classic polemic in support of a help-oriented juvenile court system, the chief probation officer of the Cook County juvenile court (that was exhibit A for Judge Mack's opti-mism) was already suggesting that some delinquents were too far de-veloped for juvenile court treatment.

Stating that the youths who were too much trouble for juvenile justice were mature and sophisticated provided a good jurispruden-tial rationale for not extending the protection of a youth-oriented policy. If the worst cases for a young people's court were significantly more adult in their cognition and behavior than other young offenders and most youths of the same chronological age, the reasons that justify special treatment of youths might not apply.

The problem with withdrawing the protections of juvenile justice only when the subject is mature and sophisticated is that the most serious cases are not the most mature offenders. The empirical pattern is, if anything, to the contrary. The most serious acts of violence are committed by youths with lower levels of educational attainment, less capacity for mature judgment, and less understanding of the world around them than others of the same chronological age (the research is discussed in chapter 7). The limited number of studies conducted suggest that serious violence was always an important prediction of waiver to adult court (see Eigen 1981b).

Furthermore, the statutes that provide automatic transfer for listed serious crimes of violence for offenders above a particular age contradict the theory that maturity is the animating principle behind transfers to criminal court. The recent tendency to reduce the age for transfer if the offense is sufficiently serious clarifies the priorities that operate generally in juvenile court protections. Whereas youths who are near the age boundary of juvenile and criminal court may be pushed up because of age, in most cases it is the severity of the offense that is the major influence. Youths who are immature are no less dangerous for that reason. Youths who are dangerous are no older. The traditional language about maturity and sophistication was always largely a cover story for pushing the worst cases into criminal courts. The recent emphasis on serious violence has simply removed the cover.

Thus there is no persuasive reason to assume that legal policy for youths is irrelevant to policy for violent young offenders. This does not mean that violent youths should be treated no differently than nonviolent youths. It does mean that why the legal system wishes to treat some young people who violate the law differently than older law violators must be surveyed and discussed before proper legal responses to youth violence can be framed.

Rationales for Distinctive Youth Policies

Little has been written about the substantive reasons that support a separate policy for crimes committed by young offenders for a variety of reasons. As described in the first section, part of the problem is that debate about procedures and jurisdiction crowd out substantive content. Part of the problem is that juvenile and criminal court issues are usually considered separately, so that little pressure is exerted to examine the same questions across different procedural settings. And part of the problem is that separate treatment of children seems intuitively right in a way that does not invite further scrutiny from its advocates. Of course, youths who violate laws should be treated differently than adults; should we imprison 6-year-olds? Legal nuance and complexity might seem beside the point in this context. For these reasons, no sustained analysis of the factors that justify separate treatment of adolescent offenders is in the literature to measure against the known facts on serious youth violence.

Some years ago, I suggested two general policy clusters that were at work in youth crime policy: diminished responsibility because of immaturity and special efforts designed to give young offenders room to reform in the course of adolescence. The issues grouped under the former heading relate to the traditional concerns of criminal law, so that these matters tell us why a criminal lawyer might regard a younger offender as less culpable than an older offender. The cluster of policies under the latter heading are derived from legal policies toward young persons in the process of growing up.

Dimensions of Diminished Responsibility

To consider immaturity as a species of diminished responsibility has some historic precedent but little analytic history. Children below the age of 7 were not responsible in common law for criminal acts by reason of incapacity, whereas those between 7 and 14 were the subject of special inquiries. Capacity in this sense was an all or nothing matter, like legal insanity, rather than a question of degree. Yet the logic of diminished culpability argues that even after a youth passes the minimum threshold of competence, this barely competent youth is not as culpable and therefore not as deserving of a full measure of punishment as a fully qualified adult offender. Just as a psychiatric disorder or cognitive impairment that does not render a subject exempt from criminal law might still justly mitigate the punishment to be imposed, so a minimally competent adolescent does not deserve all of an adult's punishment for the same act.

This notion of diminished culpability is not an isolated element of juvenile jurisprudence but rather one expression of a core value in

Anglo-American criminal law, the idea of penal proportionality. This conception is no less central to modern criminal law just because it is difficult to express with precision.

> During the past two-and-a-half centuries, a persistent strand in liberal thought relating to penal justice has been the notion that the severity of criminal penalties should be limited by and proportioned to the culpability of the offender and his offense. In the United States the concept of penal proportion has even found its way into constitutional doctrine, notably that concerned with prohibitions against cruel and unusual punishment. It is an idea notoriously difficult of definition and application: the meaning of culpability and the measurement of its degree elude mathematical precision and therefore produce controversy and conflict. (Allen 1996:42–43)

The absence of analysis about penal proportionality for early and middle adolescents is a particular puzzle. Despite the universal acceptance of immaturity in doctrines of infancy and the widespread acceptance of reduced levels of responsibility in the early teen years, there has been little analysis of the aspects of immaturity that are relevant to mitigation of punishment. Again, the intuitive appeal of the result and the separate categories of juvenile and criminal jurisprudence may have deferred analysis of its rationale. Yet the specific attributes of legal immaturity must be discovered before judgments can be made about what ages and conditions are relevant in reducing punishment on this ground.

In an important sense, the entire delinquency jurisdiction of the juvenile court can be seen as an institutional expression of the diminished culpability of youthful offenders, but this is at best mute testimony, lacking any statement of principles that can be analyzed and criticized. Furthermore, when this concept of proportionality is expressed only in the institutional output of one court system, the transfer of offenders from juvenile to criminal court risks changing the applicable penal principles without justification.

What characteristics of children and adolescents might lead us to lessen punishment in the name of penal proportionality? An initial distinction needs to be drawn between diminished responsibilities and the poor decisions such impairments encourage. Most teenaged law violators make bad decisions, but so do most adults who commit major infractions of criminal law. Anglo-American criminal law is designed to punish bad decisions at full measure. But persons who, for reasons not their own fault, lack the ability observed in the common citizen either to appreciate the difference between wrong and allowable conduct or to conform their conduct to the law's requirements may be blameless because of their incapacity. Even when the offender has sufficient cognitive skill and emotional control to pass the threshold of criminal capacity, a significant deficit in the ability to appreciate or control behavior would mean that the forbidden conduct is not *as much* the offender's fault, and the quantum of appropriate punishment is less.

How might 14- and 15- and 17-year-olds who commit crimes be said to exhibit diminished capacity in moral and legal terms? There are three different types of personal attributes that influence adolescents who may lack full adult skills and therefore also full adult moral responsibilities. First, older children and younger adolescents may lack fully developed cognitive abilities to comprehend the moral content of commands and to apply legal and moral rules to social situations. The lack of this kind of capacity is at the heart of infancy as an absolute defense to criminal liability. The ability to comprehend and apply rules in the abstract requires a mix of cognitive ability and information. A young person who lacks these skills will not do well on a paper-and-pencil test to assess knowledge about what is lawful and unlawful behavior and why. Very young children have obvious gaps in both information and the cognitive skills to use it. Older children have more subtle but still significant deficits in moral reasoning abilities. For most normal adolescents, the ability to reason in adult style is present by age 16 (Steinberg and Cauffman 1996).

A second skill that is required to transform cognitive understanding into the capacity to obey the law is the ability to control impulses. This is not the type of capacity that can be tested well on abstract written or oral surveys. Long after a child knows that taking property is wrong, the capacity to resist temptation may not be fully operational. To an important extent, self-control is a habit of behavior developed over a period of time, a habit dependant on the experience of successfully exercising it. This particular type of maturity, like so many others, takes practice. Whereas children must start learning to control impulses at a very early age, the question of how long the process continues until adult levels of behavioral control are achieved is an open one. Impulse control is a social skill not easily measured in a laboratory. We also do not know the extent to which lessons to control impulses are generalized or how context-specific the habits of self-control are. Children, for example, must learn not to dash in front of cars at an early age. How much of that capacity to control carries over when other impulses—say, the temptation to cheat on a test—occurs in new situations? The assessment of self-control in field settings is not a thick chapter in current psychological knowledge. The developmental psychology of self-control has been studied by question-and-answer hypotheticals and not by the observation of behavior in natural settings.

There may also be an important distinction between impulse control in the context of frustration and impulse control for temptation. If so, the frustration context may be the more important one to study for the determinants of youth violence. When should we expect adult levels of control of violent impulses while one is angry? Almost certainly the developing adolescent can only learn his or her way to such control by experience. This process will probably not be completed until very late in the teen years.

To the extent that new situations and opportunities require new habits of self-control, the teen years are periods when self-control issues are confronted on a series of distinctive, new battlefields. The physical controls of earlier years are supplanted by physical freedoms. New domains—including secondary education, sex, and driving—require not only the cognitive appreciation of the need for self-control in a new situation but also its practice. If this normally takes some time to develop, the bad decisions made along the way should not be punished as severely as those of adults who have passed through the period when the opportunity to develop habits of self-control in a variety of domains relevant to criminal law has occurred. To the extent that inexperience is associated with poor decisions, it is partially excusable in the teen years, whereas it is not understandable in later life.

The ability to resist peer pressure is the third social skill that is not fully developed in many adolescents. A teen may know right from wrong and may even have developed the capacity to control his or her impulses if left alone to do so, but resisting temptation while alone is a different task from resisting the pressure to commit an offense when among adolescent peers who wish to misbehave. Most adolescent decisions to break the law or not take place on a social stage, where the immediate pressure of peers is the real motive for most teenage crime. A necessary condition for an adolescent to stay law-abiding is the ability to deflect or resist peer pressure. Many youths lack this crucial social skill for a long time.

Figure 5.1 shows the percentage of juvenile defendants who were

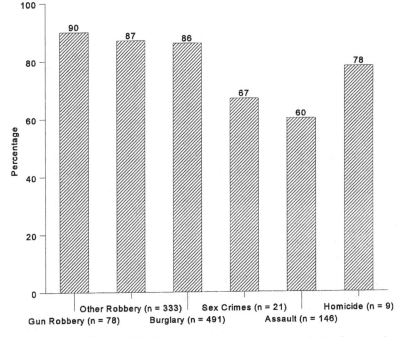

Figure 5.1. Multiple Offender Cases as a Percentage of Total Juveniles Charged, by Crime, New York City. Source: Zimring (1981).

accused of committing a crime with at least one confederate in the New York City juvenile courts in the 1970s, as discussed in chapter 2. These offenders were all under 16 years of age when the act was committed. The percentage of total defendants who acted with a confederate ranged from 60 percent for assault to 90 percent for robbery. These are conservative estimates because cases in which a confederate was not caught or charged are not classified as group crimes.

The cold criminological facts are these: The teen years are characterized by what has long been called group offending. No matter the crime, if a teenager is the offender, he or she is usually not committing the offense alone. When adults commit theft, they are usually acting alone. When youths commit theft, they usually steal in groups. When adults commit rape, robbery, homicide, burglary, or assault, they are usually acting alone. When adolescents commit rape, robbery, homicide, burglary, or assault, they are usually accompanied by others (Zimring 1981). The setting for the offenses of adolescents is the presence of delinquent peers as witnesses and collaborators.

No fact of adolescent criminality is more important than what sociologists call its group context. And this fact is important to a balanced and worldly theory of adolescent moral and legal responsibility for criminal acts. When an adult offender commits rape, his motive may be rage or lust or any number of other things. When a teen offender in a group commits rape, an important part of the motive is usually "I dare you" or its functional equivalent, "Don't be a chicken." When an adolescent robs, steals, breaks into a house, or shoots another youth in the company of co-offenders, one real motive for this act is responding to the pressure of the explicit or implicit "I dare you." Fear of being called chicken is almost certainly the major cause of death and injury from youth violence in the United States. "I dare you" is the reason that "having delinquent friends" both precedes an adolescent's own involvement in violence and is a strong predictor of future violence (Elliott and Menard 1996; Howell and Hawkins 1998).

The capacity to deflect or resist peer pressure is a crucially necessary dimension of being law-abiding in adolescence, one that requires social experience. Youths who do not know how to deal with such pressure lack effective control of the situations that place them most at risk of crime in their teens. This surely does not excuse criminal conduct. But any moral scheme that gives mitigational recognition to other forms of inexperience must also do so for a lack of peer management skills that an accused has not had a fair opportunity to develop. This is a matter of huge importance, given the reality of contemporary youth crime as group behavior.

I do not want to suggest that current knowledge is sufficient for us to measure the extent of diminished responsibility in young offenders or to express in detail the types of understanding and control that are important parts of a normative developmental psychology. We have an awful lot of social psychology homework ahead of us before we understand the key terms in adolescent behavioral controls relevant to criminal offenses.

There are, however, two important points to be made about age and diminished responsibility even in the current state of partial knowledge. First, the ages at which the legal system can expect adult-level abilities depend on the range of experience that is regarded as important. If only the cognitive capacity to make judgments in paper-and-pencil exercises is important, adolescents are usually well equipped by their sixteenth birthdays (Steinberg and Cauffman 1996). But if social experience in matters like anger and impulse management and a fair opportunity to learn to deal with peer pressures is necessary, expecting the experienced-based ability to be fully formed before the age of 18 or 19 would seem to be wishful thinking. Becoming an adult is a gradual process in modern industrial societies. Ironically, the process may start earlier but still take longer to complete than in earlier eras (Zimring 1982:Chap. 2). Partial responsibility for law violations may come at a young age. Full responsibility will take longer.

Second, inconsistent assumptions about maturity in a range of legal contexts is a sign of trouble. In recent decades, the age of majority for such matters as gun purchases and unlimited driving licensure has been going up. Both national and state policy clearly repudiated the 18-year-old alcoholic beverage age that many states adopted after lowering the voting age. Are these trends consistent with lowering age boundaries for full penal responsibility? On what account?

It is also important to recognize that diminished responsibility is not merely a doctrine of juvenile justice but also a principle of penal proportionality. The nature of adolescent immaturity would raise many of the same issues we now confront in juvenile justice even if all young offenders were tried in criminal courts. Even if there were no separate youth policy to consult in making decisions about young offenders, their just punishment would be a separate moral and legal problem.

Room to Reform

The notion that children and adolescents should be the subject of special legal rules pervades the civil, as well as criminal, laws of most developed societies. A multiplicity of different policies is reflected in different legal areas, and there are important differences throughout law in the treatment of younger and older children. Under these circumstances, to refer to "youth policy" generally risks misunderstanding both the subjects of the policies and the policy objects of the rules.

The policies I refer to in this section concern adolescence, a period that spans roughly the age of 11 or 12 to about age 21, the only segment of childhood associated with high rates of serious crime. This span has been described as a period of increasing semiautonomy when youths acquire adult liberties in stages and learn their way toward adult freedoms along the way (Zimring 1982).

At the heart of this process is a notion of adolescence as a period of learning by doing, when competence in decision making can be achieved only by making decisions and making mistakes. For this reason, adolescence is a period that is mistake-prone by design. The special challenge here is to create safeguards in the environment of adolescents that reduce the permanent costs of mistakes. Two goals of legal policy are to facilitate learning by doing and to reduce the hazards associated with expectable errors. One important hallmark of successful adolescence is survival to adulthood, preferably with one's life chances intact.

A popular theory about the etiology of youth crime provides a rationale for room to reform policy. The theory is that the high prevalence of offenses in the teen years and the rather high rates of incidence for those who offend are transitory phenomena associated with a transitional status and life period (Elliott 1994; Moffitt 1993). Even without heroic interventions, the conduct that occurs at peak rates in adolescence will level off substantially if and when adolescents achieve adult roles and status.

That assumption carries three implications. First, it regards criminal offenses as a more or less normal adolescent phenomenon, a byproduct of the same transitional status that increases traffic accidents, rates of accidental pregnancy, and suicidal gestures. This view of youth crime tells us, therefore, that policy toward those offenses that are a byproduct of adolescence should be a part of larger policies toward youth. A second implication is that major interventions may not be necessary to reorient offenders. The central notion of what has been called adolescence-limited offending is that the cure for youth crime is growing up (Moffitt 1993).

Third, there is the worry that drastic countermeasures, those that inhibit the natural transition to adulthood, may cause more harm than they are worth. If a particular treatment risks severe side effects, it should be elected only if failure to use it would risk even more. Those who regard youth crime as a transitional phenomenon believe that problems of deviance will resolve themselves without drastic interventions, and they doubt the efficacy of high-risk interventions on utilitarian grounds. So juvenile justice theories with labels like radical nonintervention and diversion are a natural outgrowth of the belief that long-term prospects for most young offenders are favorable.

But what about the short term? The current costs of youth crime to the community at large, to other adolescents and to the offenders themselves are quite large. How would advocates of nonintervention protect the community? Is a room-to-reform policy inconsistent with *any* punitive responses to adolescent law violation?

The emphasis in youth development policy is on risk management over a period of transitional high danger. As we have seen, the legal theory that adolescents are not fully mature allows a larger variety of risk management tactics than are available for dealing with adults. Minors cannot purchase liquor, acquire handguns, buy cigarettes, or pilot planes. Younger adolescents are constrained by curfews and compulsory education laws. There are special age-graded rules for driving motor vehicles, signing contracts, and entering into employment relationships. Many of these rules are meant to protect the young person from the predation of others. Many are meant to protect young people from themselves. Many are meant to protect the community from harmful acts by the young. So there is a rich mixture of risk management strategies available to reduce the level of harmful consequences from youth crime.

Does this mix of strategies include the punishment of intentional harm? The answer to this question is yes from all but the most extreme radical noninterventionists, but attaching negative consequences to youthful offenders is regarded as good policy only up to a point. Youth development proponents are suspicious of sacrificing the interests of a young person to serve as a deterrent example to other youths if the punished offender's interests are substantially prejudiced. In fact, punishing young offenders in ways that significantly diminish their life chances compromises the essential core of a youth protection policy. There may be circumstances in which drastic punishment is required, but it always violates important elements of youth development policy and can be tolerated rarely and only in cases of proven need. In this view, punishment is suspect when it compromises the long-term interests of the targeted young offender.

A Categorical Exception for Violent Crime?

We must now inquire whether any of the considerations in the previous section are relevant to the legal treatment of youth violence. The argument against extending special youth-oriented policies to violent crime goes something like this: It is okay to allow soft treatment of young offenders when the crimes they commit are kid's stuff, but violent crime is not kid's stuff. There is no room for leniency. Because the harm is so serious, young offenders should be treated just as if they were adults.

The threshold question to be considered here is whether this reasoning amounts to a principled argument against special youth policies for all violent young offenders. That is, should violent acts be excluded from the scope of the policies just discussed? There is no logical basis for limiting the scope of a mitigation principle because the harm caused by the criminal act is great. Doctrines of diminished responsibility have their greatest impact when large injuries have been caused by actors not fully capable of understanding and self-control. The visible importance of diminished responsibility in these cases arises because the punishments provided for the fully culpable are quite severe, and the reductive impact of mitigating punishment is correspondingly large. But if the doctrine of diminished responsibility means anything in relation to the punishment of immature offenders, its impact cannot be limited to trivial cases. Diminished responsibility is either generally applicable or generally unpersuasive as a mitigating principle.

The situation with a room-to-reform perspective is more complicated. Young offenders do not become any less young because they pull the trigger that ends a human life, and the victim is just as dead as if shot by an adult. The seriousness of the harm intended and done may push legal policy in the opposite direction. But this countervailing force is not the same as suggesting that either violent acts or the young persons who commit them are not suitable candidates for a youth-oriented policy.

To begin with, violent crime *is* kid stuff as an empirical matter if American criminology is to be trusted. The high prevalence of violence by male adolescents is a central finding of chapter 2. Just under half of all males report being responsible for an assault at some time during their teen years. So a very large proportion of the male population crosses the border into violence at least once in adolescence. Furthermore, teen boys are involved in assaults at annual rates ranging from 10 percent to 27 percent, depending on how the term "assault" is defined and limited. African-American boys reported serious assault rates of 36 percent per year (Farrington 1998:5), and at least half involved weapons or injuries (Elliott 1994).

The empirical literature reports that violence is kid stuff in one further respect. Over 75 percent of those in Elliott's national youth survey who committed a violent offense during their teenaged years did not do so again (see Howell and Hawkins 1998:2). The majority of self-reported offenders are adolescence-limited. These are the transitional offenders who, proponents of a room-to-reform strategy believe, will outgrow criminal conduct without drastic intervention. On the evidence from self-report studies, there is no basis for a categorical exclusion of violent offenders.

Official police statistics tell a somewhat different story. A much smaller percentage of the youth population is identified as violent. But the mode in police statistics is for no repeat offense of violence among those who were ever arrested. The desistance probabilities for violence offenders are no worse than for nonviolent offenders. The only real basis for differentiating the violent offender is the seriousness of the crime, although using the offenses that young offenders are arrested for to screen for seriousness does not work well. Assaults and robberies vary tremendously in seriousness and, these two offenses account for 94 percent of all youth violence arrests.

Categorical generalizations about offenses other than homicide are a poor basis for any policy that excludes room to reform. Instead, discussion should be organized around specific subcategories of violent offenders when measuring the justice and efficacy of particular policies.

Personal Injury and Youth Policy

The kind of damage that youth violence sometimes causes means that the stakes are high when formulating policy to respond to it. Life and limb are the largest concerns in criminal justice generally, and life-threatening violence demands priority (Zimring and Hawkins 1997). But violent crime is not the only life-threatening behavior that challenges youth policy in current circumstances, nor even the most dangerous. Even though driving privileges are withheld until mid-adolescence, the learning period of unsupervised driving in the United States is associated with high risks of death and injury and large aggregate losses. From the standpoint of the community at large, the risks generated by drivers aged 16 to 21 are of similar kind and magnitude to those associated with intentional injuries.

The analogies between traffic injuries and assaultive injuries in modern American life are instructive if incomplete. In each case, the instrumentalities and values of the larger society play an important role in defining the risk environment associated with youth. Youths must learn to drive to be adults in the United States, and this imperative generates a high transitional risk that cannot be avoided. Yet improvements in the risk environment of driving in general—the kinds of roads, the kinds of cars, and the range of legally required safety precautions—can reduce the death toll. The nature of American youth violence has similar links to larger social phenomena. Distinctively high rates of lethal violence for all age groups are associated with our high rates of youth violence. Handgun availability in the general society is linked to handgun availability in the youth population, even when we attempt to prohibit it.

Why, then, are there few serious proposals to radically redefine youth traffic regulations, to defer driver's licenses until age 21, or to revoke them permanently when youths have accidents? The recent restrictions on the range of driving privileges for new drivers in California is a small and controversial step, allowing driving in less hazardous circumstances before full privileges are granted at night or with teen passengers. Why not have many more sweeping crackdowns on teen drivers in the style of recent youth crime legislation?

The transitional risks associated with young drivers may be regarded as part of the American system, a cost associated with a social process we approve. Youth violence, in contrast, is not believed to be a part of an American system that carries positive benefits. We do not think of high homicide rates as the result of the availability of firearms to the general public or the rewards of male aggression. Traffic accidents are also problems that we believe are caused by kids like ours. Youth violence is perceived as a cost imposed on American society from without.

The different social construction for traffic fatalities and assault fatalities is only one of the many differences between highway deaths and homicides. I do not mean to argue that the American public should regard the two problems as equivalent. But it is important to note that in both our history and current affairs, there are contexts in which we are willing to pay the price of adolescent development into adulthood even when community safety is at risk.

Conclusions

There are two reasons why criminal acts by immature offenders are treated differently from the same acts committed by adults. Diminished responsibility comes from a concern in criminal law about punishment in just proportion to culpability. Preserving the future life chances of young offenders comes from policies that provide special support to adolescents in the transition to adulthood. Doctrines of diminished responsibility seek to reduce the amount of punishment that is appropriate. Room-to-reform policies address not so much the amount of punishment imposed as the kind of punishment and the kind of consequences that should be avoided. The orientation of such policies is qualitative rather than quantitative.

This chapter's final contribution was a negative one. There is nothing in the known facts about adolescent violence or in other legal policies toward youths that would exclude violent injury categorically from either mitigation or protection. These policies need to be balanced against other important interests in making decisions in specific cases. One appropriate way to explore the balancing processes is to address the particular problems discussed in the following three chapters.

Firearms Policy
for the Young

The most alarming statistics about recent American youth violence concern the increasing rate of homicide, which is wholly the result of increasing gun use in assaults. During the eight years after 1985, when the homicide rate for persons over the age of 24 did not increase, the total homicide rate attributable to juvenile offenders more than doubled. But this statistic was itself an aggregation of two quite divergent trends. Juvenile homicides committed by all means other than guns were remarkably stable throughout the 1980s and the early 1990s. As we saw in chapter 3, however, the rate of gun killings resulting in the arrest of an offender under 18 years of age more than tripled over a nine-year period.

The usual pattern in the United States had been that firearms were used in a smaller percentage of homicides by adolescent offenders than in homicides by adults. In less than a decade this pattern was reversed, with a larger proportion of homicides by offenders 14 to 17 than by adults (Zimring 1996). The increase in adolescent homicides in the United States was all guns, and the public perception about this facet of contemporary youth violence was consistent with the facts.

The public attitude about gun ownership by adolescents is a rare island of consensus in the United States, where any other issue relating to firearms control is not merely controversial but also explosively contentious. The United States is a country where membership in the National Rifle Association has traditionally been regarded as a political asset for a presidential candidate. Unrestricted access to guns and ammunition is a matter of intense ideological importance to many citizens, a sentiment expressed in the phrase "firearms freedom." Academic journals publish statistical arguments that increasing the number of ordinary citizens allowed to carry concealed guns in public will reduce the homicide rate (Lott and Mustard 1997)—a conclusion that organized gun-owning groups regard as obvious and embrace with enthusiasm. The current Congress of the United States is closely divided on the question of whether the prohibition of semi-automatic firearms currently labeled assault weapons should be repealed as an obvious mistake.

But there is no support for the "firearms freedom" of 14-year-olds to buy handguns, even among groups otherwise opposed to legal restrictions on gun ownership and use. The first federal law that singled out classes of citizens forbidden to purchase firearms in the United States was passed in 1938, and minors under 18 years of age were among the first groups forbidden to acquire guns. There was no controversy associated with that exclusion at the time, and there has been no sustained effort to remove this prohibition (Zimring 1975). The federal Gun Control Act of 1968 raised the minimum age for handgun acquisition to 21, in one of the least controversial changes wrought by an otherwise contentious legislative restructuring of federal gun control that took place in two installments a generation ago (Zimring 1975). State and local laws frequently parallel the federal standard. By a strict statistical count, persons under the age of 21 are probably 90 percent of all the people prohibited from purchasing handguns in the United States in 1998. On the arithmetic, then, gun control in America is mostly about children and youths.

Although minors are prohibited from acquiring handguns, gun laws have never been an important part of youth policy in America, and policy regarding young persons has never been a significant element of federal gun law enforcement until quite recently. A 346-page summary entitled *Understanding Juvenile Law* was published in 1997 (Gardner 1997). The terms "firearms" and "guns" are not to be found in either the table of contents or the index. My earlier review and analysis of *The Changing Legal World of Adolescence* (Zimring 1982) has no mention of firearms, guns, or gun control. Alcohol and tobacco, in contrast, were each the subject of sustained coverage. Age restrictions on the acquisition of handguns were ignored in the literature because they were regarded as noncontroversial and unimportant until quite recently.

Public policy for armed juveniles is still noncontroversial, but it is far from unimportant. The sharp increase in gun woundings and killings attributed to persons under the age of 18 has been the subject of extensive media attention. The armed juvenile offender has become a priority target for state and federal legislatures since the late 1980s, including changes in criminal court transfer (discussed in the next chapter) and special provisions for crimes, gang gun crimes, and driveby shootings.

The range of legislative proposals is extraordinarily broad, and new ones are frequently ingenious and often incoherent. During the past decade, the U.S. Congress has contributed to constitutional history with two separate versions of what was entitled a Gun-free Schools Act. The first version was passed in 1989. The federal power for this act was explicitly based on congressional power to regulate commerce. The law had been patterned after federal "drug-free schools" legislation that combined the symbolic denunciation of worrisome crime with the hope that the threat of federal prosecution would reduce the presence of guns and narcotics in schools.

The U.S. Supreme Court invalidated a prosecution under the Gun-free Schools Act in *United States v. Lopez* (115 S.Ct. 1624, 1994), ruling that even the federal government's extensive powers under the commerce clause, which had been held to be almost infinitely elastic in more than fifty years of Supreme Court jurisprudence, could not be stretched to justify the extension of federal jurisdiction to the vicinities of local schools under the congressional recitals of the 1989 act. The swift response of Congress was to pass another Gun-free Schools Act in short order, with different factual recitals to justify federal jurisdiction. Whether any of this activity helped to keep America's schools gun-free is not known. But the flurry of extensive legislative activity in the national government was a poignant contrast to the previous century, when the gun-free status of primary and secondary education was not an issue.

Borrowings

One frequently used technique for creating legislation to combat adolescent gun use was to appropriate countermeasures that had been popular in other contexts. Just as Congress dusted off the approach of the Drug-free Schools Act to create gun-free schools, the advocates who had combined long, mandatory prison sentences and baseball terminology to pass a "three strikes" initiative in the state of California started a campaign that would have provided a mandatory ten-year prison term for any person 14 years of age or older convicted of unlawfully carrying firearms (Podger 1995). While the effort to place this proposal on the initiative ballot failed, a cut-back version was passed by the state legislature with the enhanced mandatory penalties for older juveniles intact.

The aim of this chapter is to provide a strategic context for thinking about adolescent gun use as a public policy problem. A first step is to consider the justification of age-specific prohibitions. Why deny handguns to adolescents when we allow them to adults? Do the assumptions we make when we prohibit youths from having guns limit the extent to which we can punish them for violating the prohibition? These are the concerns of the first section.

The second section discusses the potential and limits of partial or age-specific prohibition as a gun control strategy. How much harder is it to keep guns from felons and minors when most other citizens can have all the guns they want? What types of controls should be imposed on qualified gun owners to deter transfers to the prohibited subjects?

The third section examines the practical problems of prohibiting gun access to the young by examining the record of parallel efforts to restrict access to tobacco, alcohol, and pornography. Is age-specific gun prohibition likely to be easier or more difficult to accomplish? The final section discusses a more particularized topic: whether juvenile courts or criminal courts are better suited to handle adolescents charged with the violation of age-specific gun prohibitions.

Minimum Ages: Justifications and Implications

A disadvantage often associated with widespread social policy consensus is the absence of any searching analysis of its justification. Ninety percent of the people prohibited from acquiring handguns in the United States are currently under the age of 21, yet little of the literature on gun regulation concerns the reason for this ban. However, the reason may be inferred from the terms of the regulations in force, as well as by comparing the restrictions imposed on other disqualified groups, although a fair amount of license needs to be taken in the interpretation of existing statutes.

Restrictions on minors are the joint product of ambivalence about widespread and unrestricted handgun ownership and a consensus judgment that middle and even late adolescents are not sufficiently mature to be trusted with easily concealed lethal weapons. One common characteristic concerning goods and services that by law cannot be purchased by those below a specific minimum age is anxiety about the easy access of adults to these items. We enforce minimum age restrictions on vices such as gambling, drinking alcohol, and smoking in part because we are uneasy with the notion of free access to these activities for anyone.

A minimum age is an interesting kind of compromise between prohibition and free access, in which mixed feelings about a behavior produce restrictions designed to protect children and youths. As a historical matter, this can be seen in the strenuous enforcement of minimum ages for alcohol in the decades after Prohibition was repealed. A more recent example of this kind of projection has been the increased focus on keeping cigarettes from children and youths as the social status of smoking has declined in the 1980s and 1990s. Yet another example is the crusade against child pornography that absorbed the energies and passions of groups that were really opposed to hard-core pornography in general (Hawkins and Zimring 1989:176–179).

A similar type of ambivalence played an important role, not in the 1938 minimum age for all firearms, but in the 1968 minimum age of handguns. The objective justification for singling out handguns was their higher rate of use in homicides, suicides, and other crimes. But there was a subjective dimension as well. The handgun has a social reputation as a more dangerous weapon than a shotgun and rifle. This problematic social reputation also explains the invention of the term "Saturday night special" to describe cheap handguns and their special regulation (see Zimring 1975).

But why single out persons under the age of 21 for special restrictions? The justification for this is youthful immaturity rather than youthful malevolence. The same federal gun law that prohibits the young from acquiring handguns also bans the acquisition of firearms by convicted felons. The latter ban is permanent in the sense that the disability is never removed. The ban on youth is temporary, suggesting that the reason for the prohibition will be outgrown as the subject grows older. It can therefore be inferred that the disabling characteristic of the young is immaturity, a lack of judgment and experience that presumably would help an adult gun owner to control impulses to use the gun in an unjustified violent act.

An important distinction can be drawn between immaturity of a kind that is used to justify firearm prohibition and one that would denote the lack of moral and cognitive capacity required for minimum levels of criminal responsibility. Irresponsibility is an extreme condition, one that would rarely be found in a normal adolescent aged 14 and above. Various levels of immaturity, while they escalate the risk that members of the group will behave inappropriately, fall

far short of the disabilities that would render individuals not accountable to the criminal law. If immaturity is a head cold, irresponsibility is the equivalent of double pneumonia.

There is thus no inconsistency in denying a privilege to a high-
risk population and then punishing members of the prohibited class
when they violate the terms of the prohibition. Because we believe
that 15-year-olds are immature, we can prohibit them from acquiring handguns. If they acquire handguns nonetheless, the immaturity
that justified the age-specific prohibition does not forbid their punishment. In this sense, an age-related prohibition may be simultaneously paternalistic and punitive and not be incoherent for that
reason.

The legal regulation of youth violence becomes incoherent when
the age-specific prohibition on guns is justified because of immaturity but the claim is then made that the 15-year-old who gets hold of
a gun and then uses it in a robbery should be punished to the same
extent as a fully responsible adult for the same offense (see, e.g., the
proposal described in Podger 1995). The inconsistency here is in ignoring the diminished capacity to conform to adult standards of
judgment and risk management that is the basis for restrictions on
handgun acquisition and ownership. To make the claim for equal
culpability is to imagine that an offender is simultaneously (1) disadvantaged by a developmental process not of his or her making, and
(2) is in full possession of adult levels of maturity and judgment.

Adolescents are not the only group disqualified from gun ownership on the grounds that unrestricted access to firearms would
be dangerous. The other important exclusion in federal law is the
convicted felon (Zimring 1975). So the question arises whether convicted felons, excluded from gun ownership because of irresponsibility, should not also benefit from doctrines of diminished responsibility when they obtain guns and misuse them? Any argument that
minors and felons should be treated in a similar fashion would be
problematic on a number of grounds. The most significant is the failure to comprehend the distinction between minors and adults. Children and adolescents are excluded from gun ownership because they
cannot be expected to exercise the judgment and control that make
gun ownership a risk worth taking. But the deficiency in judgment is
not wholly the adolescent's fault, nor do we expect maturity that
early in life.

Criminals are disqualified from eligibility for gun ownership because previous criminal acts suggest an unacceptably high risk that
future gun ownership will produce trouble. We impose the same ex-

pectation of maturity on adult felons as on other adults. It is therefore appropriate to assess a punishment for conviction of criminal acts without discounts attributable to notions of diminished responsibility. The capacities of the adolescent, in contrast, more resemble those of persons over the age of majority who are prohibited from gun purchase because of a mental disease or defect. In such cases it is not a bad decision but the lack of a fully adult capacity to make decisions that is the basis for the prohibition. In each case, the impairment of capacity argues for a reduction in punishment from the full adult standard.

Wide Versus Deep Regulatory Power

The developmental immaturity that justifies much more extensive state regulation of the access of adolescents to guns also limits the extent to which offending adolescents may justly be punished for violating gun laws or for committing other crimes. An inability to impose the most severe punishment on adolescent violators might cause some reduction in the extent to which punishment can control adolescent gun crime. However, the substantial portfolio of additional powers held by the state in regulating adolescent access to guns more than compensates for the need to reduce the punitive bite of the criminal law. In jurisdictions in which adult access to weapons is substantially unregulated, the special powers available to the state to enforce gun restrictions for minors are considerable. The width of regulatory controls over adolescents in the 1990s is really quite substantial. Young persons may be stopped and searched in schools, school lockers may be examined with or without consent, private living space may be searched with parental consent, and access to guns through legal means can be prohibited. Since substantial punishment can also be imposed upon conviction of a crime, including a gun law violation, the loss of penal efficacy is not great. On balance, the tools available to limit gun misuse among the young in the United States are more substantial than those tools available to regulate the ownership and use of guns by adults.

The Prospects for Partial Prohibition

To say that the prospect for restricting the availability of guns to minors is superior to the prospect for regulating adult use is by no means the equivalent of concluding that age-specific gun controls in

the United States work well. Gun control for any target group is difficult to accomplish in an environment where available handguns
might exceed 60 million.

There are three different ways in which young persons prohibited
by law from obtaining firearms may nonetheless got them, and an
effective age-specific prohibition must reduce the availability of
weapons in all three sources of supply. The first avenue is the legally
regulated retail suppliers, who account for the bulk of the transfers of
new weapons in the United States, and many used guns as well. This
is the regulated market. Second, there is the unregulated exchange of
used guns between individuals in what has been called the hand-to-
hand market (Zimring and Hawkins 1987). I include in this category
the transfers that occur through theft, as well as sales and gifts between individuals who are not dealers. The persons who originally
owned the weapons before transfer were lawfully in possession of
their guns, but the transfers were not regulated and did not result in
any records that linked the new owners with the guns. This channel
of supply can be called the gray market. The third method of supply
involves the bulk purchasing of guns followed by their sale to persons who the seller knows are not legally permitted to own them.
The people in this business are dealers in an illegal market. I refer to
this channel of supply as the black market in guns.

The distinction between the black and gray markets often depends
on the sellers' knowledge that a weapon transfer is a crime. In a gray
market, gun owners do not specialize in the transfer of weapons to
prohibited owners. Instead, there are transfers of privately owned
guns to a wide variety of different kinds of users at market rates and
without any regulatory formality. In black market transactions, in
contrast, sellers supply goods to people they know cannot legally
possess them. The price charged for the illegal transfer will be somewhat higher than the market rate that the legally qualified person
would be willing to pay because there is a crime tariff, a premium to
compensate the seller for the risk that boosts the price on the black
market.

Any effective program to keep handguns from minors needs to develop strategies to cut off these rather different kinds of supply
mechanisms. This means that any successful program of age-specific
prohibition must fight a war simultaneously on three distinct fronts.
Also, different methods of regulation and policing will be needed for
these different channels of supply.

The regulated market for the sale of handguns is a very easy place to secure compliance with minimum age regulations. Gun dealers are instructed to require proof of a prospective buyer's age, and photo identification on such documents as drivers' licenses is widely carried and easily consulted. The age on a driver's license can, of course, be forged, but even then prospective buyers might look too young to be thought 21 until shortly before they attain the age of legal possession. If law enforcement puts regulatory pressure on dealers to exercise caution, legitimate retail channels can be effectively closed to underage buyers without great effort.

This ease of administration is a happy contrast to the problems in preventing retail sales to convicted felons. Documentary proof of age can be found in the purse or wallet of most adult citizens. Documentary evidence of the absence of a criminal record is not something a citizen carries. For decades, federal law was frustrated by the fact that only a sworn statement by the purchaser about the absence of a disqualifying record was required. The provision in the so-called Brady bill of 1993 to require a waiting period, as well as notification to a prospective purchaser's hometown police department or an instant check of the purchaser's criminal record, was an attempt to close a gap for felons that did not exist for underage buyers.

Preventing the gray market supply of handguns to minors is more difficult and more costly than securing compliance in the regulated market. More used guns are acquired by transfers from individuals than from dealers (Newton and Zimring 1969). The law could require the same documentation and reporting from private individuals as from dealers. Enforcement of this requirement would be a problem, however, because dealers are repeat players in the gun transfer business who have strong incentives to learn and observe the rules, whereas individuals are not. They are difficult to reach through official communications and hard to motivate except with the threat of draconian penalties. Of course, record checks are not likely in the sale of stolen weapons. As hard as it might be to motivate a casual gun owner to check the credentials of a purchaser, obtaining cooperation from a burglar or fence would be harder still.

Whereas regulatory efforts are the principal resources used to secure compliance from retail dealers, trying to reduce the flow of guns to youths in the gray market should involve a mixture of regulatory and criminal law enforcement. The more success a regulatory campaign achieves, the more reasonable it will be for law enforcement authorities to assume that careless sellers are not totally innocent. That is, if most hand-to-hand transfers are casual and undocumented, it will be hard to single out a seller for moral condemnation and criminal prosecution; but if general standards of care about minimum age are high, the sellers who violate those standards will be easier targets.

Reducing gun availability in black markets is principally the task of criminal law enforcement strategies and personnel. The black market dealer is in an illegal business and is therefore a hopeless candidate for regulatory exhortation. Supply reduction in black markets will resemble narcotics law enforcement, with buy-and-bust campaigns and the use of informers. This kind of criminal law enforcement is labor-intensive. Because of the high cost, the level of priority that policing authorities must assign to black market guns to produce stringent enforcement will be very high and thus rarely found in local police departments or in police agencies of general jurisdiction. Only firearms specialists such as the Federal Bureau of Alcohol, Tobacco and Firearms and specialized police subunits (so-called gun squads) will engage in sustained black market countermeasures.

Varieties of Supply Conditions

Although gray market and black market channels are found in many urban environments, their use as a source of supply for minors will probably vary with the level of general availability in a jurisdiction. Where gun availability is high, the gray market would be a much more important source of guns for youths than the black market. With very large numbers of handguns widely distributed in the population, there are many more guns to be casually transferred. The chance that a random burglary will produce a handgun to be sold or converted to the adolescent housebreaker's personal use is much higher when 40 percent of the households in a city have handguns than when only 10 percent do. This larger supply of gray market guns would make it correspondingly easier for a 16-year-old who wanted a gun to find it. Furthermore, there is also a much greater chance that teenagers will have access to handguns taken from their own homes. Thus, it would be difficult for black marketeers to charge substantial premium prices to underage customers. The gray market, then, would be a dominant if not exclusive source of supply.

With low general handgun availability, however, there will be fewer gray market guns for youths to borrow, to buy, and to steal. Then the black market will be a more important channel of supply to the underage customer. In places like New York City and Boston, where the proportion of households with handguns is believed to be much smaller than in cities like Atlanta, Houston, and Miami, more resources should be devoted to black market countermeasures and fewer to policing and regulating the gray market. In high availability areas, the gray market will require a larger fraction of enforcement effort.

The distinction between high availability and low availability cities should alert us to the probability that efforts to keep firearms from youths are hostage to the general condition of gun availability. As hard as it might be to reduce the black market availability of handguns in low-ownership cities like New York and Boston, it would seem harder still to reduce gun availability to youngsters in high-ownership cities like Atlanta, Miami and Houston.

Prevention Versus Apprehension

Two different but complementary law enforcement goals are the re-duced supply of guns to youths, and the removal of prohibited weapons from young persons who carry or possess them. The ulti-mate aim of each strategy is to reduce the level of firearm violence committed by minors. The obvious advantage of preventing youths from obtaining guns in the first place is that no risk of gun violence will be run if the youth population is never armed. To the extent that prevention programs succeed in keeping youth populations gun-free, a prohibition policy is operating at maximum efficiency. But preven-tion programs are far from perfect, so that a second line of defense in-volves generating programs that try to discover and remove firearms unlawfully in the possession of minors. The target population for a prevention program should include anybody who might be part of a supply chain of weapons to minors, including adult gun sellers and owners. The targets of apprehension programs that try to remove guns from prohibited underage owners are limited to young people under the age of eligibility for ownership.

Programs designed to apprehend illegal gun possessors and re-move their guns are less effective than prevention programs in one respect but more effective in two other dimensions. The disadvan-tage of a removal strategy is that the high-risk population spends some time in possession of guns. An apprehension effect may come after the fact of gun violence. The advantage of apprehension strate-gies is that the population of guns and to a lesser extent of persons who have to be screened is smaller. To cut off market sources of supply to young persons, one has to regulate the commerce in all the weapons that are the subject of the prohibition, not just those weapons that are eventually acquired by minors. A removal strategy, in contrast, is only interested in those guns that are in fact illegally possessed. Whereas the search for illegal weapons will involve screening and inconveniencing many young people who are not carrying guns, it will inconvenience very few adults. The particular beneficiaries of the shift in emphasis from prevention to apprehension will be adult gun owners and sellers. The second efficiency of gun removal strategies is that when a minor is apprehended while carrying a loaded gun, the risk that he or she was headed for trouble is usually quite high. The proximity to social harm of an adolescent who is carrying a gun on the street means that successful apprehension leads to lower rates of gun violence in the immediate future.

The same environmental conditions limit the effectiveness of both prevention and removal strategies. If guns are freely available, preventing a teenager from acquiring one particular gun can easily be neutralized by alternative sources of supply. The salutary impact of removing a gun from a youth may also be short-lived if the confiscated weapon can be easily replaced. For this reason both handgun prevention and removal should be easier to implement successfully in conditions of low handgun availability.

There may also be a relationship between the level of general handgun availability and the optimal mix of prevention and apprehension strategies in the enforcement of a minimum handgun age. Very high levels of handgun availability can frustrate both prevention and apprehension, but not in equal measure. Cutting off a few sources may have only a slight impact on the availability of guns to youths in a high-availability environment. High availability will also frustrate gun removal programs, but the apprehension of youths with guns will still reduce gun violence during the period immediately following the apprehension, a period when the immediate risk of adolescent gun violence may be quite high. Thus the comparative advantage may lie with programs that emphasize gun removal in high-availability environments. Furthermore, if high availability spills over to higher levels of adolescent gun carrying and use, the same number of police searches will turn up many more guns. So the unit cost of gun apprehension, ironically, is reduced by the very circumstances that frustrate the overall effectiveness of a gun removal strategy.

The foregoing analysis suggests two hypotheses. First, both prevention and apprehension will be more effective in restricting gun violence by minors in environments of low handgun availability. Second, strategies aimed at removing guns possessed by adolescents will be emphasized to the detriment of prevention programs in conditions of high availability. Neither hypothesis has been put to a rigorous test.

Other Minimum Age Regulations

Whereas preventing minors from carrying handguns was an unimportant chapter in the legal regulation of youths until quite recently, efforts to restrict the availability of other substances and privileges have been a substantial undertaking in the United States and other developed nations. Two major government efforts that have attempted to enforce relatively high minimum ages have involved alcohol (typically age 21) and tobacco (typically age 18 but going up). What does the history of these regulations teach us about the prospects of age-specific handgun prohibition?

State efforts to enforce a minimum age for tobacco and alcohol have not produced black markets in the sense of ongoing businesses devoted to illegal sales, mostly because of the ample supply of cigarettes and alcohol diverted from ordinary channels of commerce. Until quite recently there was not even much gray market activity fueling the supply of cigarettes to middle adolescents. State and local regulation of tobacco purchases was so lax that most adolescents who wanted to obtain cigarettes could purchase them through ordinary retail outlets.

State efforts to enforce minimum age limits for alcohol were much more substantial than for cigarettes. Beverage control authorities typically issued special licenses to businesses that wished to sell alcohol for consumption on the premises or to take home. Enforcing age limits in on-site locations such as bars and restaurants is relatively easy because the consumers are visibly present to be inspected by proprietors, and enforcement authorities can monitor the compliance of businesses by direct observation of the premises.

However, keeping alcoholic beverages sold in bulk form at package stores from being diverted to underage consumers is a much more difficult proposition than keeping them out of bars. The principal gray market diversions of alcoholic beverages sold at retail to qualified purchasers are: (1) theft or borrowing from home liquor supplies by minors, (2) social sharing of alcohol by those just over the legal age with their younger acquaintances and dates, and (3) planned purchase by those over the drinking age of quantities of alcohol intended for the sole or joint use of minors. Similar gray market opportunities exist for tobacco, and the recent increase in regulatory resources to reduce direct sales to minors will probably shift underage supply from over-the-counter sales to gray market channels.

The analogy between handguns and either alcohol or cigarettes is incomplete because there are differences between the substances and in the social context of commerce. Guns are a big-ticket item, with a high purchase price, whereas typical quantities of alcohol and cigarettes are lower priced. Handguns have a reputation for danger and carry some stigma, whereas cigarettes and alcohol do not. Firearms are also durable goods. Having a gun does not generate a high frequency of resupply needs, even for ammunition.

Even allowing for such differences, the history of attempts to enforce minimum age requirements for alcohol provides important insights for those who want to reduce the gray market for guns. For alcohol, gray markets of supply depend on social patterns of interaction. Unless teenagers are raiding the liquor cabinet of their or some other family, the age of social peers and their willingness to help are the key variables that make alcohol relatively easy or relatively hard to obtain.

Twenty-one-year-old males comingle with 19-year-old males at work and in school, and they date girls who are 17 and 18 years old. Thus alcohol will be easily available to those who regularly participate in social groupings with persons old enough to make retail purchases. Without rigid social boundaries between different age groups, the effective age limit for a particular behavior may be somewhat lower than the formal limit and significantly influenced by patterns of social interaction in late adolescence and early adulthood.

One frequent impact of this gray market phenomenon is that minimum age restrictions tend to screen out more effectively much younger adolescents (e.g., 13-, 14-, and 15-year-olds) than those who are closer to the age border. The more that the prohibited good is distributed by near peers, the larger the increment of effectiveness to be expected among the very young. If alcohol is chiefly obtained from home liquor cabinets, 15-year-olds and 19-year-olds will have equal access to supplies. If the primary source of beer is friends or friends of friends, the 15-year-old will have a much harder time obtaining alcohol than the 19-year-old. If the chief source of gray market guns is social acquaintances, it will be much easier for 19-year-olds than for 15-year-olds to obtain guns when the minimum age is 21. Under such peer supply circumstances, the adult suppliers who must become the primary target of enforcement efforts are not all that different from the young persons they supply.

There is another context in which social circumstances and expectations might be critical determinants of adolescent handgun acquisition, an aspect that drug and alcohol analysts frequently call the demand side. If possession and use of alcohol or a drug have high status for social peers, the odds increase that a particular adolescent will obtain and use it. The positive status of the substance has a sort of double-whammy effect, making younger persons more anxious to obtain it and older persons more willing to supply it.

The social status and meaning of handguns in adolescent cultures should be an important determinant of the rate of handgun ownership and use. To some extent this may be a matter of the perceived need for self-defense in some circumstances. But social status is a powerful incentive for adolescent behavior, independent of any need for lethal forms of self-defense. Those who wish to predict and explain adolescent behavior in utilitarian terms should never forget the overwhelming value of social standing among peers to most adolescents.

Negative peer attitudes can have an immediate and substantial impact on adolescent gun violence. The steep increases in gun homicide after the mid-1980s (reported in chapter 3) provides frightening evidence of how quickly changes in fashion can generate community consequences. The good news may be that attaching negative stigma to gun use will have immediate and substantial impact. The bad news is that attaching negative stigma to risk-taking behavior among adolescents is no easy task. A generation of antismoking propaganda in the United States has had its least consistent and least dramatic impact on teenage smoking trends. If the objective of a public information campaign is to give risk taking a bad name, teenagers will be a particularly hard sell—all the more reason for the social values of adolescence to be a priority target for any public information campaign that seeks to reduce the risk of lethal violence.

Juvenile or Criminal Court?

If a campaign to reduce firearms violence is going to be an important element in the general response to youth violence, it is worth considering whether juvenile courts or criminal courts provide the best institutional setting. It will not always be possible to choose between these settings because juvenile court jurisdiction is almost always over by age 18, whereas the existing framework of federal and most state laws tries to enforce a minimum age of 21 for handguns. The very oldest gun law violators will only fit into the jurisdiction of the criminal court, and this is also the court best suited to hear criminal charges against persons over the age of 18 who are apprehended while trying to sell guns to minors.

But which is the best court system for offenders under 18 who possess and carry loaded guns on city streets? Addressing this question has both theoretical and practical value. As a practical matter, such cases are not rare events in the 1990s, and an increasing emphasis on disarming juveniles can be expected to increase the volume of weapons cases whether or not teenage armaments increase. Therefore, where best to process such cases is a matter of immediate practical importance. The theoretical value of discussing the superior court setting for gun cases is that it provides a specific context in which to debate the merits of alternative processing strategies. To isolate the major law enforcement problems being generated by youth violence, to consider them one at a time, reduces the sweeping generalizations found in debates about juvenile versus criminal courts. Greater specificity in subject matter might reduce the margin of error in policy analysis.

What might be the advantages of referring 14-, 15-, 16-, and 17-year-olds, arrested for carrying loaded handguns, to the jurisdiction of the criminal courts? First, criminal courts have the power to impose longer periods of secure confinement on persons convicted of crime than are available in the juvenile courts. But the practical value of greater sanctioning power is much more important in cases of shootings and serious injuries than of carrying concealed weapons and possession. Frequently the maximum punishment available for the latter charges will be less than the duration of confinement available in juvenile court. Also, because the juvenile weapons violator is competing with older offenders and more serious crimes in criminal court, there is no a priori reason to believe that the sanctions imposed on 15-year-olds who possess guns will be even somewhat more serious than the treatment those same cases would receive in a juvenile court.

Second, armed juveniles are serious cases and it is often argued that serious cases belong in the jurisdiction of the criminal court. Pete Wilson (1997), the governor of California, seems to be making this argument when he asserts, "Juvenile Court was not designed to deal with youth who commit serious and violent crime . . . or kids who carry assault weapons" (p. 1). Implicit in this view is the notion that referring young offenders to juvenile court trivializes the offense. This is really an objection to juvenile court jurisdiction for *any* serious offense, and it might apply with greater force to the tens of thousands of violent assaults and robberies referred to the juvenile courts each year. If delinquency jurisdiction is a bad idea for any serious misbehavior, it would be a bad idea for gun cases. But the empirical foundation of this point of view is not strong. Rather than imbue marginal cases with seriousness by association, mixing juvenile cases into the adult system might have the reverse effect, a possibility that was just mentioned in connection with criminal court sanctions (see Greenwood et al. 1980).

The comparative advantages of the juvenile court for gun cases come from that court's long history of coping with status offenses. A law that denies handguns to all below a certain age and punishes those who defy it is called a status offense because the behavior is forbidden only because of the offender's youthful status. A large proportion of juvenile court business during the entire century of its existence has been the enforcement of age-defined status offenses, including underage drinking, smoking, driving, and violating curfews. Whereas some status offenses like smoking are violations of laws motivated solely by the desire to protect the minor, a substantial number of the traditional status offenses administered by the juvenile court also involve protecting the community against dangerous behavior by the immature. Certainly the enforcement of juvenile curfews and underage drinking restrictions have community protection as a justifying objective.

It thus appears that the enforcement of minimum age gun laws involves a close fit to the strategies and procedures of juvenile courts in a high volume of other types of cases. One remarkable characteristic of the current discussion is that the continuity between gun countermeasures and traditional status offense enforcement has gone unnoticed. The fit with tradition here is not a dispositive argument for the continuation of jurisdiction by juvenile courts in gun cases. It is, however, both remarkable and disturbing when public dialogue about appropriate responses in gun cases takes place without reference to a century's experience in closely related domains.

But debating whether juvenile courts or criminal courts should do the heavy lifting in adolescent gun control is also asking the wrong question in a demonstrably important way. The social context of adolescent gun markets and behavior demonstrates that significant effort will be necessary on both sides of any age boundary between juvenile and criminal courts before a coherent strategy can be executed. More important than choosing between competing court systems is a consensus on common principles and a coordination of effort that can effectively harness both institutions to a common strategy.

SEVEN

"That Malice
Which Is to Supply Age"
Standards for Transfer
to Criminal Court

[A] boy of ten years old was convicted on his
own confession of murdering his bedfellow,
there appearing in his whole behavior plain to-
kens of a mischievous discretion; and, as sparing
this boy merely on account of his tender years
might be of dangerous consequences to the
public, by propagating a notion that children
might commit such atrocious crimes with im-
punity, it was unanimously agreed by all the
judges that he was a proper subject of capital
punishment. But, in all such cases, the evidence
of that malice which is to supply age, ought
to be strong and clear beyond all doubt and
contradiction.

Sir William Blackstone (1857)

For the most part, the border between the jurisdiction of
the juvenile court and the criminal court is a matter of
chronological age. If arrested offenders are below the maximum jurisdictional age of the juvenile court when an offense is committed,
they are referred to the juvenile court and accused of delinquency. If
the offenders are above the jurisdictional age boundary, they are accused of a crime and processed by the criminal court. In most states,
this age boundary is the eighteenth birthday, but in some jurisdictions it can be as young as the sixteenth birthday.

A system that allocated defendants between juvenile and criminal
courts solely on the basis of chronological age would be tidy but
risky. Since their beginning, most systems of juvenile justice have

also provided for the transfer of some defendants below the maximum age to criminal courts. The accused most at risk for transfer were those who were believed to be unsuitable for juvenile court adjudication because of a lengthy juvenile court record, because they were accused of a very serious offense, or because they were just below the maximum age (see Rothman 1980:285). There were other reasons to transfer a subject to criminal court, and there are minor crimes like vice arrests for which the accused would prefer the consequences in criminal court. For the most part, however, transfer to criminal court has meant denying the accused the protection of the court for children. The effect of this is to put the transferred defendant at risk of greater punishments and restraints than are available in the juvenile justice system.

The current concern with juvenile violence has produced a flood of legislative activity designed to increase the number of violent offenses by juveniles that qualify for transfer to criminal court. In large part, this stance is a specific type of get-tough strategy that is more focused on increasing the punishment for such offenses than in fine tuning the niceties of court jurisdiction. But something more than the wish for greater punishment is at work. Between 1992 and 1995, forty American states relaxed the requirements for transferring an accused under the maximum age of jurisdiction into criminal court (Torbet et al. 1996), yet only three states lowered the maximum age for juvenile court jurisdiction. If the strategic mission was to get tough on as many juvenile offenders as possible, a downward shift in jurisdiction maximum age would have vastly more impact on adolescent offenders than relaxing the standards for transfer to criminal court for specific offenses. However, the latter is a popular law reform strategy because the most serious cases of youth violence are also the types of offenses that the public believes are most suited to the processes and sanctions of the criminal court. The public believes that the minimum punishment deserved by the offender in these deep-end cases of juvenile violence greatly exceeds the ordinary sentencing powers of a juvenile court.

This chapter is about the efforts to identify appropriate cases for transfer to criminal court. The first section discusses judicial waiver or transfer of juvenile offenders in traditional juvenile justice systems. The second section examines recent legislative efforts to define the circumstances of the charge and age that should lead to automatic jurisdiction in criminal court. The third section contrasts rules and discretion as the instrumentalities used to control decisions about transfer. The fourth section compares the prosecutor and the juvenile court judge as discretionary authorities in decisions about transfer. The final section explores the irony of extensive changes in the framework of judicial waiver in the 1990s without any real dissatisfaction with how the system is working.

My conclusion is that case-by-case determinations for making transfer decisions are far superior to binding categorical rules, so that extensive discretionary power is necessary in transfer decision making. For this reason, the real choice is not between rule-based and discretionary selection but rather between prosecutorial discretion and judicial discretion. Furthermore, the nature of the decision is sufficiently similar to criminal sentencing so that judges are better suited to the task than prosecutors.

Judicial Waiver in the Juvenile Court

Age alone has never been the only criterion for the jurisdiction of the juvenile court. From the beginning, juvenile court judges could waive jurisdiction over subjects young enough to be processed by the court in ordinary circumstances, and this "waiver of jurisdiction" allowed prosecution of a minor in a criminal court. When the formal jurisprudence of the juvenile court emphasized the treatment of delinquency, the official reason for waiving jurisdiction was often that the juvenile was not suitable for or amenable to treatment. As the court's rationale has become more eclectic, the official reasons for passing juveniles onto the criminal courts have become somewhat more diverse. Studies of judicial waiver have highlighted such factors as the seriousness of the offense, being in the top age group for the juvenile court, and the extensiveness of the prior record (see Dawson 1992; Eigen 1978 and 1981a).

The traditional waiver decision was made by the juvenile court judge because the juvenile court was given original jurisdiction over all youths who were within the court's age range. Before prosecuting attorneys played a major role in juvenile court proceedings, the question of waiver was raised by the court on its own initiative or with the assistance of court probation staff. After public prosecutors became a fixture in juvenile court proceedings, it was typically a prosecutor who proposed that a particular accused juvenile be transferred and the judge who made the dispositive judgment (see Dawson 1992).

The standards that were said to govern individual waiver decisions were anything but rule-bound in a number of respects. First, the decision was described as discretionary in character, thus inviting the judges to use a wide variety of criteria in individual cases. Also, there was often no requirement for written justification of a particular choice or for any reasoned elaboration of how the many factors of potential relevance had been balanced.

It should come as no surprise that a considerable gap opened up between the doctrinal characteristics that were supposed to govern waiver decisions and the actual circumstances that did so. Age, maturity, and demonstrated nonamenability to treatment were the sort of characteristics that might most comfortably explain a decision to push a subject out of juvenile court in a regime where treatment was the dominant rationale of a court for children. But the seriousness of the offense was probably a much more powerful predictor of waiver than a solely rehabilitative orientation would ever allow. In Joel Eigen's study of waiver in Philadelphia (1978 and 1981a), for example, half of all homicide arrests and only 2 percent of all robbery cases produced waiver decisions.

The ad hoc and discretionary nature of judicial waiver decisions was neither a secret nor an accident. Judicial discretion unfettered by rules or principles more concrete than "the best interests of the child" was supposed to govern all the decisions of juvenile court judges. Waiver cases were simply one more example of the hegemony of discretion in the juvenile court. Yet the serious consequences of waivers and the fact that discretion was linked to a rejection of the juvenile, rather than treatment or protection, made judicial discretion in waiver cases appear more problematic than that in other matters. Discretion to waive seems more like a decision to punish than to protect a youth. It is thus no accident that the fist successful challenge to judicial power in the juvenile court on constitutional grounds concerned a hearing to decide about the waiver of an accused in which the juvenile was not represented by counsel (*Kent v. United States*, 383 U.S. 541, 1966).

In theory, judicial waiver of jurisdiction was available to the juvenile court whether or not the criminal court wished to take jurisdiction, and the motivations for waiving jurisdiction could be of many different kinds. In practice, most judicial waivers of jurisdiction fit one of three case profiles. The first was a juvenile charged with a crime so serious that the minimum level of punishment felt to be necessary was greatly in excess of the sanctions available to the juvenile court. Most of these cases were crimes of violence, and murder was the offense most frequently followed by judicial waiver. A second group of cases involved juveniles with extensive records of arrest and juvenile court sanctions who had exhausted the patience of a juvenile court judge when rearrested. The third category was close to the age boundary that separates juvenile and criminal courts. For this category, the juvenile's already advanced age might also have reduced the amount of secure confinement that could have been imposed by a juvenile court because the youth was that much closer to whatever age was the outer limit of juvenile court power.

It is customary to lump together all these very different kinds of waiver cases together into a single category and to investigate the effects of waiver procedure on the aggregate. This kind of analysis will typically find that the majority of all cases are property offenses and that punishments in the criminal court are less severe than the sanctions that would have been available to a juvenile court. But the reason for such conclusions is an inappropriate aggregation: Very different cases with very different waiver consequences are lumped together.

The very oldest juveniles may be transferred to criminal court because the juvenile court judge feels that the defendant is appropriate for an adult forum, independent of any expectation of a more severe punishment. Some offenders close to the age boundary will request transfer to criminal court in such cases as prostitution and gambling in which it is likely to be less punitive. For different reasons, multiple recidivists expelled from the juvenile court may also benefit from seeing a new judge in a new court. They also may benefit from the lack of an adult criminal record when the same charge might resemble the top of a very high mountain in the defendant's juvenile court record (Greenwood et al. 1980).

But severely violent cases put the juvenile at risk of much longer confinement. Eigen (1981a) found long prison terms, including life imprisonment, in his sample of juveniles waived for homicide charges and quite lengthy terms of imprisonment for waived robbers. A more recent study estimated that criminal court processing of violent cases produced term lengths five times as great as those that would have been available in juvenile court (see Howell 1996). The homicide sentences in Eigen's sample were longer for waivered juveniles than for the average adult, although the comparison did not control for the different types of homicide found in the two age groups. Thus the impact of waiver on punishment in cases of high seriousness is profound.

The not insubstantial empirical literature on the effects of discretionary waiver supports four conclusions. First, the consequences of transfer vary substantially with the type of case. Substituting criminal for juvenile court can be expected to produce a wide range of different punishments, from substantially more lenient to much more severe. Second, the increased punishment associated with waiver is most pronounced in crimes of the greatest seriousness. Felony murder and firearms robbery cases will produce substantial escalation in sentences when the criminal court, with its larger powers, takes control. Third, waived violence, as a category, can produce very substantial escalation in punishment in the criminal courts.

This last conclusion should be qualified because it may not apply to the full range of violent felonies committed by adolescents. The small number of violent offenses waived into criminal court by judicial selection are probably clustered near the very top of the seriousness scale for youth violence. This is also where the punishment between juvenile and criminal courts will be most substantial. Transferring large numbers of nonfatal assaults and typical adolescent street robberies will certainly diminish the large difference between sanctions for violent cases. It would be an error of high magnitude to expect that the behavior of criminal courts in assault cases would produce punishment differences of the kind noted in murder prosecutions.

Because the sample of violent cases is both small and selective, the existing data on punishment in the criminal courts do not show that mitigations associated with youth and immaturity fail to influence sentencing decisions. On the one hand, at least in those cases that do not produce life sentences, even the extended prison terms found in current research could have reflected a mitigating consideration of the defendants' youth. The way to determine this would be to compare adult and waived juvenile sentences for similar crimes of serious violence. On the other hand, some of the data we do have on criminal court sentencing of serious violence places a rather low upper limit on the mitigatory influence of a defendant's youth.

The Policy Significance of Small Numbers

The fourth often-confirmed empirical finding on waiver is an important preliminary to any consideration of law reform. Every study of judicial waiver by metropolitan court systems has found that cases waived from juvenile to criminal court by judicial discretion are small both in absolute numbers and as a proportion of those cases eligible for waiver consideration.

The best actuarial data come from am empirical study of Texas cases published by Robert Dawson in 1992. The study reports the incidence and characteristics of judicial waivers that occurred during the fiscal year September 1987 through August 1988. There were 14,150 felony charge referrals to Texas juvenile courts in that year, and each such referral could have produced a motion by the prosecutor to transfer the juvenile and a waiver determination by the presiding juvenile court judge. A total of 112 motions to waive were filed by local prosecutors that year, a rate of 8 filings for every 1,000 felony charges. Juvenile court judges granted waiver in 87 of the 112 cases, so that the statewide rate of consummated transfer to the criminal court was 6 for every 1,000 felonies.

The rate of waiver is lower in Texas in 1987–1988 than in many other jurisdictions, partly became of the low age of maximum jurisdiction. Juveniles mature out of the Texas system on their seventeenth birthday, one year earlier than in most jurisdictions. A lower maximum jurisdictional age reduces the volume of likely waiver cases in three ways. First, a large age cohort normally found in the juvenile court is missing. Adding 17-year-olds onto the court's jurisdiction would increase the volume of crime by 20 percent to 30 percent. Second, 17-year-olds appear more adult than other clients in the juvenile court and thus would be at greater risk of judicial waiver for that reason. Third, the rate of life-threatening and homicidal violence is higher among 17-year-olds than among any other age group under the typical jurisdiction of the juvenile court (see chapter 2). Thus, adding all the 17-year-olds to a juvenile court population in the state of Texas would substantially increase the number of serious cases of violence that carry the greatest risk of waiver.

Furthermore, waiver requests may have been lower in Texas during the period of the Dawson study because a new "blended jurisdiction" statute was just becoming effective in September 1987. As shown in chapter 10, the availability of this blended alternative has not restrained the increase in transfer over the long term, but some short-term influence may have been present. The eighty-seven transfers during the study period were lower than calendar year totals reported for 1984 to 1986 by 25 percent (Texas Juvenile Probation Commission 1984–1986).

Table 7.1 shows the rate of prosecutorial motions to waive and judicial granting of waiver for seven categories in Texas during the fis-

Table 7.1. Rate of Waiver Motions and Waiver Outcome by Offense, Texas, Fiscal Year 1988

	Motions Filed as Percentage of Cases	Motions Granted as Percentage of Cases
Homicide (96)	31.00	27.00
Robbery (478)	6.10	4.00
Sex assault (380)	2.90	2.10
Aggravated assault and attempted murder (948)	1.50	1.10
Drugs (614)	1.00	0.70
Burglary (6,367)	0.19	0.15
Other	1.00	0.50

Source: Dawson 1992, Table 4, p. 988, and Table 28, p. 1013.

cal year 1988. The largest contrast is between homicide charges and everything else. Thirty-one percent of the ninety-six cases of homicide referred to the Texas juvenile court were the subject of prosecutorial waiver motions, and 27 percent of all homicide charges resulted in judicial waiver; this is five times the motion rate of the next highest crime category and seven times the rate at which motions to waive are granted in the next most frequent offense. During the study period, Texas courts granted waiver in one out of every twenty-five robbery charges, one out of every fifty sexual assault charges, and one out of every ninety cases of nonfatal aggravated assault (including attempted murder).

Even though the actuarial probability of waiver is slight for the Index crimes of violence, the chance that violent crime charges will generate a transfer is much greater than for property and drug offenses. During the study period, the successful waiver rate in drug cases was 7 per 1,000 felony charges; for burglary it was less than 2 per 1,000. None of the more than 1,000 felony theft charges produced a motion to waive, and the waiver rate for motor vehicle theft was slightly above 1 in 1,000 cases.

This study shows both the importance of the violence category to the general issue of transfer and the inadequacy of this label as a complete explanation. Homicide cases are vastly more likely to be transferred to adult courts than other crimes; yet almost three-quarters of the homicide charges are retained in the jurisdiction of the juvenile court. The three Index crimes of violence other than homicide account for less than 20 percent of the felony caseload of the juvenile court; yet they constitute the majority of motions to waive jurisdiction in nonhomicide cases in Texas. The actuarial chances of waiver for nonfatal offenses of violence vary from 1 percent to 4 percent. Thus it is easy to be misled about the extent to which offenses of violence "explain" prosecutorial and judicial decisions to waive. The violent crime is close to a necessary condition for waiver, in that no other crime category has waiver rates as great as 1 percent. But no charge category, not even homicide, seems to be close to a sufficient condition for predicting a waiver.

Explaining Low Incidence

In Dawson's (1992) data, a low rate of prosecutorial requests for waiver is the major explanation for the tiny proportion of felony charges that produced waiver in Texas. But there are indications that the judiciary, as well as the prosecutors, applied strict standards in waiver cases. More than 20 percent of these requests were denied in the sample year, and the rate of judicial rejection was much higher than that in Dallas, the county where the rate of waiver requests from the prosecutor was the highest. The low rate of prosecutor requests reflects, to some extent, the standards that prosecutors anticipate from judges. So it is best to view the low rates of waiver as the joint product of prosecutorial and judicial standards.

However, actuarial statistics like those in table 7.1 strike many observers as astonishing. Only 1 in 100 aggravated assaults resulted in waiver? Only 1 robbery charge for every 25 lodged in the juvenile court? Only 27 percent of all homicide charges in juvenile court transferred to criminal court? The statistical profile that emerges appears to be more than lenient when the transfer statistics we have been reviewing are measured against popular images of premeditated murder, predatory robbery, and sexual assault. Why is this?

The transfer statistics in table 7.1 actually tell two different stories, with the pattern for homicide cases being very different in its implications for policy than that for all other violent crimes. When prosecutors ask for transfer to criminal court in more than 30 percent of all cases, it appears that homicide charges by the police are frequently the cause. Killings by older juveniles, felony-related homicides, cases in which the juvenile performed the act that caused the death rather than being an accomplice—these are likely to be the types of charges that motivate prosecutors to seek waiver. Cases that involve inactive accessories, arguments and fights in which adolescents are engaged in mutual combat, and very young defendants are apt to be overrepresented in the cluster of homicide charges that remain in the juvenile justice system. There is a substantial number of cases in which weak evidence produces either a dismissal of all charges or the pursuit of less serious charges in the juvenile court. Still, what the data in table 7.1 show is that most cases of intentional injury that causes death provoke serious consideration of transfer to criminal court by prosecutors and judges.

The rate of transfers when other Index offenses of violence are charged varies between a high of 4 percent and a low of 1.1 percent in Texas, where all felony charges can serve as a foundation for transfer to criminal court. The story that these statistics tell is that these offenses are not very close to the threshold necessary for contemplation of transfer. Robbery, aggravated assault, and evidently sexual assault are heterogeneous offense categories in which the conduct that produces the criminal charge can vary from relatively minor to life-threatening. What table 7.1 demonstrates is that the bulk of the cases of robbery, sexual assault, and aggravated assault is not close to the boundary between juvenile court retention and transfer to criminal court. It must be only the particularly aggravated forms of other than lethal assault and robbery that provoke consideration of transfer— that or random variation.

The same contrast between homicide and other crimes of violence has been found in earlier research. Eigen (1981a) estimated a frequency of transfer in Philadelphia homicide cases that was twenty-five times the magnitude of the transfer frequency in robbery cases. In his analysis of a juvenile court jurisdiction up to the eighteenth birthday, homicide charges clustered even closer to the waiver threshold, whereas robbery charges were evidently far removed from the types of acts and injuries that make transfer an obvious issue.

A visual illustration of the distribution of various violent offenses around the threshold for waiver in Texas can be produced if we assume that the seriousness of each of the four Index offenses of violence is distributed across the range of juvenile offenses in the bell-shaped curve of a normal distribution. There is no reason to suppose that such a distribution is a precise description of the variations in the seriousness of the offense in Texas, but the point being made would hold with most other distributions of seriousness. The point of these fanciful figures is the contrast between homicide, in which the waiver threshold is within 1 standard deviation of more than half of all offenses, and all the other crimes of violence, in which the point at which waiver occurs is far removed from most of the offenses.

To some extent, the opinions of prosecutors and judges about the degree of criminal harm that might justify transfer to criminal court may be a function of the particular legal test for transfer and the particular institutional environment in the juvenile and criminal courts. A change in the law is likely to somewhat alter the opinion of judges and lawyers about what sorts of juvenile criminality are appropriate for waiver. To a substantial extent, however, professional opinion about the seriousness of particular types of behavior will not change dramatically when there is a shift in statutory language or classification. Therefore, low base rates of transfer requests and motion approvals may be evidence that legislative efforts to increase criminal court transfers might encounter resistance in the juvenile and criminal courts.

Legislative Standards

Since the juvenile court is itself a statutory creation, the jurisdictional boundary between juvenile and criminal court is always subject to modification by state legislation. Indeed, as was mentioned in chapter 1, state legislation dealing with criminal court jurisdiction for juveniles has been nearly universal in the 1990s. Since 1987, every American state, except Vermont, has passed legislation encouraging the transfer of persons under the maximum age for juvenile court jurisdiction to criminal court under some circumstances (General Accounting Office 1995; Hutzler 1982; Lyons 1997; Torbet et al. 1996).

Legislative standards for the transfer of juvenile offenders can take a variety of forms. First, the legislature may stipulate only the circumstances in which a juvenile court judge is legally authorized to consider the transfer of an accused. Most states have legislation of this kind, stipulating classes of offenders by age and charge who are eligible for waiver. The legislation that specifies eligible cases is typically quite broad, sometimes allowing any charge or any felony charge and not infrequently adding a minimum age at the time the offenses was committed, for example, 14, 15, or 16. The effect is to facilitate a discretionary waiver for broad classes of cases. The only

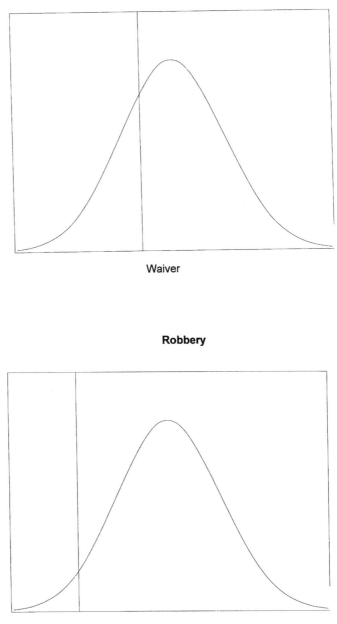

Homicide

Waiver

Robbery

Waiver

Figure 7.1. Transfer Thresholds in a Normal Distribution of the Seriousness of Juvenile Crime, Texas. Source: Dawson (1992).

Aggravated Assault

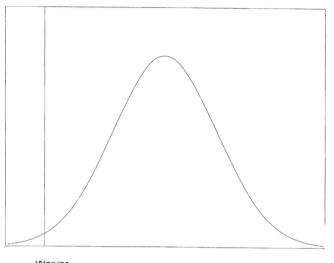

Waiver

Figure 7.1. Continued.

restrictions on judicial discretion are the classes of cases that are excluded from eligibility because of the youth of the accused or the
triviality of the criminal charge.

Second, the legislation may attempt to exert more influence on the
pattern of decision making in judicial waiver hearings by providing
for the presumption of unfitness for particular types of offenses and
offenders. In California, for example, a minor over the age of 16 at the
time of an offense who is currently charged with one of twenty-nine
felonies is presumed "not fit for juvenile court jurisdiction." The
power to make findings still resides with the juvenile court judge,
but the standard of proof has been altered to facilitate transfer in
some selected cases.

Third, some legislative rules allocate jurisdiction to the criminal
court under specified circumstances, typically serious crimes for
which the direct filing of charges in criminal court is mandated if the
accused is over a stipulated minimum age. In Colorado, for example,
defendants under the maximum age for juvenile court jurisdiction
may nonetheless be charged by direct filing in criminal court if they
are over 14 years of age and are charged with one of a legislative list
of violent crimes (Torbet et al. 1996). Mandatory legislative standards

deprive juvenile court judges of the power to consider criminal court jurisdiction. This type of legislative standard is frequently directed at murder charges and has been extended to a wide variety of felony charges in some recent state legislation.

Substantial controversy surrounds the likely effects of mandatory legislative standards. For example, Barry Feld (1987) believes that such legislative standards provide a principle of offense as the dividing line between juvenile and criminal court cases. The competition between judicial waiver and that kind of legislative standard is thus a competition between rule and discretion.

A contrasting view comes from the study of the systemic impact of changing legal rules. In this view, the effect of mandatory legislative standards is to replace the discretion of judges with that of prosecutors. Assume that a state law provides mandatory transfer to criminal court if the accused is over 14 years of age and is charged with a capital felony. This is a frequent provision in state laws and is unqualified and mandatory in its terminology. Assume further that first degree murder is a capital offense and that second degree murder and manslaughter are not. No matter what charge is lodged by the arresting police, it is the public prosecutor in the United States who has the discretionary power to determine whether and which criminal charges will be filed. A person over the age of 14, but still within the jurisdictional age of the juvenile court, is arrested for homicide under circumstances that might support a first degree murder charge. Under the statute, if the prosecutor elects to charge first degree murder, criminal court jurisdiction is mandatory. But if the prosecutor wishes to charge the defendant with second degree murder or manslaughter or any other lesser charge, the case can be referred to a juvenile court. Because prosecutors always have the discretionary power to downgrade the charge, they always have the discretionary power to divert a case that appears to be covered by a mandatory criminal court standard to the delinquency jurisdiction of juvenile court. Thus mandatory waiver provisions allow transfers at the discretion of the prosecutor.

The amount of discretion available to a prosecuting attorney in practice is a function of the number and variety of charges that are the subject of mandatory transfer legislation. If murder is the only one, the prosecutor will have independent discretion to choose the forum only in cases in which intentional injuries produce death. If there is a long list of crimes, the prosecutorial power to choose the court by selecting an appropriate charge can be very broad.

The only method available to create a system that is closer to making transfer provisions mandatory, in fact, would be one that attempted to deprive the juvenile court of jurisdiction for specific factual circumstances. But even depriving the juvenile court of jurisdiction over murder charges will not hold if the prosecutor charges homicidal crimes with less culpable mental states. Giving the criminal court exclusive jurisdiction when young people are charged with being criminally responsible for producing a death would be a standard that was more difficult to evade.

To say that mandatory transfer provisions are easy for prosecutors to evade is not the same thing as arguing that such provisions will invariably fall short of their mark. The inevitable discretionary content in transfer standards means that a prosecutor's preferences and priorities will play a large part in determining the outcome of legislative reform. But the preferences of prosecutors cannot be inferred from support of mandatory transfer laws because prosecutors derive other benefits from these laws. Prosecutors may well desire a shift in power from juvenile court judges to themselves. Prosecutors must plead and present a case to initiate a transfer to the criminal court in a judicial waiver jurisdiction. When automatic waiver provisions are in force, they can achieve a transfer with no effort. There are thus prosecutorial incentives for support of laws that may be invoked infrequently, and one can imagine prosecutors supporting expansions in mandatory transfer provisions even when they have no strong objection to the type of substantive outcome profiled in table 7.1.

The variety of incentives in automatic transfer schemes makes their impact once they are in effect harder to predict. Some prosecutors may support dramatic expansions in automatic transfer provisions because they want to revolutionize the punishment of adolescents who commit violent offenses. Others might support the same legislative reform to increase their powers and reduce their workload when transfer initiatives do occur.

Rule Versus Discretion in Criminal Court Transfers

One important indicator of the likely effects of efforts to reform juvenile justice laws is the behavior of prosecutors and judges in current circumstances. The patterns of conduct reported in table 7.1 perform double duty. They function to some extent as a baseline, a description of the status quo that should be used as a contrast to the specific ambitions of law reformers. But data on prosecutorial and judicial behavior also provide information on how prosecutors and judges might wish to respond to new rules.

Dawson's findings in 1992, for example, suggest that a shift in power from judges to prosecutors would expand the proportion of cases in which criminal court processing would be preferred, but the impact of this shift would probably be more substantial in Dallas (where the rate of requests was higher in the previous regime) than in other Texas jurisdictions. Furthermore, and of greater general significance than the county-to-county variations found in Texas, the very different waiver rates for homicide and other violent offenses predict different system responses to mandatory transfer rules for murder, on the one hand, and the remaining offenses of violence, on the other.

For homicide cases, the 31 percent prosecutorial waiver request rates in table 7.1 indicate that prosecutors strongly desired the sorts of outcomes they were achieving with transfers in one-third to one-half of all homicide charges against juveniles. This is based on the fact that they were willing to invest effort in seeking waiver in just over 30 percent of all homicide charges. A mandatory transfer law might achieve anywhere from half to nearly complete transfer by prosecutors since no effort has to be invested in other homicide cases.

In contrast, a presumption of unfitness in juvenile homicides would be expected to have a somewhat smaller impact on transfer probabilities because juvenile court judges retain decision-making power in such cases and they are somewhat more conservative than prosecutors in granting transfers in the present system. The major difference between presumption statutes and automatic transfer statutes are the continued power of juvenile courts and the requirement that a prosecutor make a motion to waive. A presumption rather than an automatic transfer would require prosecutorial effort in an individual case. This effort might not be a substantial deterrent in the one-third to one-half of all homicide cases in which prosecutors strongly desire criminal court disposition, but it would have more dramatic impact in the cluster of cases for which the prosecutor did not much care where the charge was adjudicated.

All other things being equal, an increased volume of juvenile homicides processed in adult courts should reduce somewhat the average severity of the sanctions because more cases of lesser seriousness would be in the adult court for sentencing. Less serious punishment of adolescent homicides in criminal courts might increase the rate of transfer. That is, if special provisions were made to accommodate more lenient sentences for immature offenders, this might increase the rate at which they were transferred to the criminal courts in cases close to the seriousness threshold for wishing transfer.

Unless shifting power from juvenile court judges to prosecutors makes a very substantial difference to the number of transfers that prosecutors really care about, fewer than half of all Texas juvenile homicides will have high prosecutorial priority no matter what legal standard is used. That is the lesson of table 7.1. When lower-priority cases are transferred to criminal court, the transfer outcome can be regarded as gratuitous in the sense that no strong preference existed. The best way to guard against gratuitous waivers is to require some judicial determination that the accused should be waived, perhaps with a provision that the unfitness of juveniles accused of intentional homicide should be presumed. But unless the distribution of homicide cases could be predicted by a series of detailed neutral principles, only a discretionary sorting can achieve a distribution close to that produced by the current system.

Transfer, Discretion, and Nonlethal Violence

For nonlethal juvenile crimes of violence, the only general rule that fits the pattern noted in the Dawson study (1992) would be a rule of exclusion. More than 90 percent of each class of nonlethal violence charges are not the subject of waiver motions by the prosecutor, and more than 95 percent of each category of violent criminal charges do not result in a waiver. Among the alternatives to blanket exclusion is extensive discretion, or standards that would discriminate in advance between classes of nonlethal violence. The final alternative would be a 20- to fiftyfold expansion of the number and kind of cases to be tried in the criminal courts. This would be the impact of any mandatory transfer rule that was literally followed.

The two offenses that have been the subject of the most substantial grading efforts are robbery and assault, and none of the attempts at subdivision in existing law approaches the distribution found in the Texas study (Dawson 1992). A typical subdivision of robbery would be between offenses that involve a gun or other deadly weapon and those that do not. The typical subdivision for assault would distinguish between attacks that are intended to produce or do produce great bodily harm and are committed with firearms and all other types of assault. The more specific and more serious grades of robbery and assault might become subject to automatic transfer, whereas the lesser grades do not (see, e.g., Virginia's three-tier transfer statute, S44, Chap. 914, §16.1–269.1).

There is no doubt that some general classes of assault and robbery are more dangerous on the average than others but it is equally obvious that any categories and distinctions are crude when measured against the extraordinary heterogeneity of adolescent robbery and assault.

Distinguishing between armed robbery with a firearm and other forms of robbery is an example of what can be called a vertical distinction in grading the seriousness of the crime. As a general rule, robberies that involve loaded firearms are much more life-threatening and probably more frightening to their victims than nonfirearm robberies. But only a small minority of gun robberies inflict injuries on their victims, whereas serious injuries can be inflicted by knife-wielding robbers and muggers (see Zimring and Zuehl 1986). So one problem of vertical discrimination is ranking the severity of various different combinations of weapons and personal injury. Further dimensions of seriousness in robbery involve (1) the amount of property taken, (2) whether the robbery was only attempted or successful, (3) the nature of the threat issued by the robber, (4) the offenders' age, and (5) the circumstances of the victim. Added to these problems of vertical distinction are issues of horizontal differentiation in culpability, which are inevitable in adolescent crime because of the predominance of group crime. Is the unarmed adolescent who entered a convenience store as an accessory to a gun-wielding robber more culpable or less culpable than another robber of the same age who wields a knife in a robbery but has no armed companion?

The problems of vertical and horizontal discriminations of seriousness are probably more difficult in assault than in robbery. The gradations of injury for each weapon type are huge; guns are not even fired in more than half of all firearm assaults, whereas many shootings at the other extreme are only an inch removed from murder. Was the combat mutual? Was the attack provoked? Was the attacker in fear of his victim? Writing a comprehensive account of the factors that determine the seriousness of adolescent assault is more than difficult; adding the complexity and indeterminacy of group involvement compounds the problem.

The point of this discussion can be briefly stated. Discretion is inescapably important in determining the proper punishment for the manifold varieties of adolescent violent crime. If the consequences of transfer to criminal court are to be consistent and severe, only a very few cases of juvenile robbery or assault will deserve transfer, and discretionary decisions will be necessary to select the 1 in 100 or the 1 in 25 cases from the others.

If decisions about waiver do not select the few cases that demand severe punishment from the mass of less serious incidents, extensive discretion in determining the nature and extent of punishment will be necessary in criminal court, which would be responsible for processing the bulk of adolescent violence cases in the United States. Any tribunal that has to swallow whole the vast miscellany of American youth violence might soon appear in its processes and outcomes rather similar to the modern juvenile court. Much of the variability in case outcomes in juvenile court, as well as the extensive discretion utilized in decision making, is the predictable result of the character and volume of American youth violence.

Prosecutor or Judge?

Substantial discretion is a necessary element in determining the justice system's response to violent acts by adolescent offenders. The important issue is who should decide on the particular outcome of criminal charges. The competition for discretionary power is between prosecutors and judges. To the extent that judges are the appropriate holders of discretionary power, there is the further question of whether the power to determine transfer should be given to judges of the juvenile court or of the criminal court.

The discretionary power of the public prosecutor is substantial in all criminal cases, and no realistic rearrangement of authority in juvenile or criminal courts would significantly limit the authority of prosecutors to determine and modify criminal charges. With respect to waiver, the field of choice is between systems of judicial waiver or transfer, in which the prosecutor would share power, and systems of automatic transfer, in which the prosecutorial power to choose the forum operates without judicial review. The important substantive issue is whether the transfer power is better exercised by prosecutors alone or shared by prosecutors and judges. The decisive consideration is whether the skills and perspectives of a judge improve the quality of decision in transfer cases.

Two types of argument favor allocating discretionary power to judges: considerations of competence and of perspective. If it is correct to regard the waiver question in serious crime as a particularized determination of the minimum punishment the community would tolerate, is this type of determination more within the competence of prosecutors or of judges? If the issue of minimum desert is essentially a political one, a popularly elected prosecutor might be in a better position to make such a political judgment than an appointed judge, who operates at some remove from the political sentiments of a particular community. But if the determination of just deserts involves balancing elements like the defendant's immaturity and the extent of the defendant's participation against the particular harm of the crime committed, this task seems very similar to sentencing, and judges would seem to be better equipped than prosecutors to take the substantive responsibility for sentencing decisions.

The second dimension concerns the appropriate perspective for making waiver decisions. Both judges and prosecutors are public servants, but they represent the public interest in different ways. The judicial role is umpiral, whereas the prosecutorial perspective is adversarial. The judicial responsibility is to take into account everything of relevance when making a decision on waiver. The prosecutor's responsibility is to give emphasis to those considerations that will enhance punishment and the suppression of crime. This contrast in perspective explains most of the debates about waiver policy. Those who favor judicial control over waiver favor an umpiral perspective. Once that premise is granted, a conclusion of judicial superiority is inevitable. But if one believes that a decision should enhance only the crime-controlling capacity of the system, the prosecutorial advantage is just as obvious. Without doubt an umpiral perspective is something of an impediment in maximizing the crime control potential of criminal court transfer.

If one characterizes the issue as a charging decision, the better analogy is to the charge processes that are at the center of prosecutorial power in the Anglo-American system. If one characterizes the decision as one that must determine the proper range of punishments in a specific case, the closer analogy is to a sentencing function and an umpiral perspective. This is not the same as characterizing a waiver decision in terms of whether it is offender-centered or offense-centered. Obviously, if transfer decisions were offender-centered, they would favor judicial power. But even if the major element were the character and seriousness of the offense, the proper punishment response to a specific offense might more appropriately be decided by a judge than by a prosecutor.

Juvenile Versus Criminal Court Judges

Once a division of authority between prosecutorial and judicial officers is settled, there remains the question of whether judicial power should be exercised by juvenile or criminal court judges. Historically the waiver decision was made by a juvenile court judge because that court had jurisdiction in the first instance over all charges. A statutory scheme that provides original jurisdiction for some charges in criminal court but also allows for waiver back to juvenile court gives whatever powers are granted to the judiciary to criminal court rather than to juvenile court judges. To the extent that expertise on adolescent development and culpability is an important element in decision making, an argument can be made for preferring juvenile to criminal court judges. But the choice is probably of minor significance when compared with the large differences in perspective that occur when judges rather than prosecutors exercise discretionary power.

The Juvenile Offender in Criminal Court

One benefit of restating and reforming the criteria for transfer is the revelation of the transparent need for criminal court policies to take special account of the immaturity and the special treatment needs of youths. Thus, the response of the criminal justice system to adolescent violence can only be coherent if it recognizes diminished responsibility, as well as special needs for education and treatment.

My claim is not that criminal courts need to reproduce all the youth-centered doctrines found in juvenile court. Extravagant efforts to reduce the extent to which sanctions hamper the developmental opportunities of young persons need not preoccupy the criminal court. But diminished responsibility because of immaturity is not a principle only of juvenile justice; it is at least as important in animating the decisions made by courts of criminal justice. Indeed, to the extent that the rationale for transfer to criminal court is based on the retributive necessity for substantial punishment, considerations of diminished responsibility are more apparently necessary in the retributive calculus of criminal court than in juvenile justice.

The complaint about life terms and the death penalty for crimes committed by 15-year-olds is not that these punishments are inconsistent with doctrines of juvenile justice. The problem rather is that they are inconsistent with properly detailed retributive claims that justify the transfer to criminal court jurisdiction of the most serious juvenile offenders. It is not the function of transfer to treat 15- and 16-year-olds as adults. Instead, it is necessary to confront in criminal court the specific and difficult issues presented when adolescents are charged with crimes of extreme gravity.

The legitimacy of transfers from juvenile to criminal court will thus depend on more than the criteria for selection that will be used. A system of transferring young offenders to criminal court can be no better than the quality of the outcomes for these cases.

Rebellion Without a Cause?

Even radical reconstruction of power and jurisdiction may have a limited effect on the punishment delivered to most adolescent offenders because very few of the powerful citizens in the criminal and juvenile justice systems are deeply dissatisfied with the substantive outcomes of the current system. The proportion of requests for waiver is high in homicide cases only and quite low for other charges of adolescent violence (see Dawson 1992; Eigen 1981a; Fagan et al. 1987). The concurrence of juvenile court judges with waiver requests is rather high across the board and higher still for the most serious offenses and offenders There is no sign of deep discontent with the process or the criteria that govern the transfer of jurisdiction to the criminal courts.

But how can this operational equanimity coexist with a legislative frenzy for the expansion of criminal court jurisdiction that has changed the law in nearly 80 percent of all American states in three years (Torbet et al. 1996)? How can the lack of concern by operating professionals occur at the very time that the U.S. House of Representatives passed a federal law to withhold grants-in-aid to any state that failed to provide original criminal court jurisdiction for juveniles accused of a long list of serious crimes? If the method for transfer does not produce anger and frustration for professionals in the system, including prosecutors, what circumstances have produced enough fury to energize a punitive rebellion at every level of American government toward the violent young offender?

The problem that is provoking legislative action is youth crime itself rather than any deficiencies that have been identified in the institutional arrangements that govern transfer decisions. High rates of youth violence are regarded as sufficient proof that *something* is wrong with the current policy. Whatever the problem, "getting tough" is advocated as an all-purpose solution. The debate about waiver policy is a textbook example of the short circuiting discussed in chapter 1, and high rates of juvenile crime are seen as a sufficient demonstration that legal institutions have failed. The current system for making decisions about the transfer of juvenile offenders is frequently a nonissue in the debates that lead to legislative change. High rates of juvenile violence are invoked, and *from this* it is concluded that the punishment for youth violence is insufficient, and *from this* it is concluded that criminal court jurisdiction for serious offenses would obviously be superior to a system that is never described, let alone assessed, in the argument.

This jump to conclusions explains the limits of contemporary attempts to modify procedures, as well as the breadth and vehemence of the legislative assault. It is the public's concern with youth violence that is animating legislative activity; so it is only that aspect of the juvenile court that is subject to legislative review. The operations of the juvenile court are never subject to any detailed scrutiny because alarming police statistics all by themselves are considered a sufficient condition to justify change. This short circuitry in argument may in fact protect the juvenile court from broader and more searching criticism, but the nature of the argument is no more logical because arbitrary immunity is coextensive with unjustified faultfinding. Radical changes in the institutional arrangements for responding to serious crimes of violence by young offenders should be based on a detailed assessment of how the current system works.

Not all silly laws have deleterious effects. The same operating personnel whose opinions counted for so little in the legislative process may collaborate with newly empowered prosecutors to minimize the operational change that new legislation will produce. Even so, the most recent generation of legislation is discouraging. First, the process was poorly informed, and a low standard of information can be dangerous in the legislative process. Second, if the actions of prosecutors, defense counsel, and judges neutralize many of the aims of the current legislation, the gap between practice and theory in criminal justice will grow wider. This gap is a major problem in its own right. Finally, a particular sadness is associated with eras of legislation when damage control is the highest ambition of the reformer.

Adolescents Who Kill

The teenager accused of criminal homicide is the worst case in a system that seeks to protect young offenders and to preserve their opportunity for normal development into adulthood. Causing a death is inflicting the greatest harm that crime can cause in a developed nation, a type of loss that the economic resources and insurance mechanisms of a rich nation cannot protect against or meaningfully compensate. If death is caused by intentional infliction of a serious injury, the youth who inflicted the injury will often have intended enough harm so that his or her moral culpability would have been great even if death had been avoided. In such cases, the combination of high levels of personal culpability and the worst-case outcome puts maximum pressure on the legal system to generate extensive punishment. Dealing with homicide is an important and particularly difficult part of a comprehensive policy toward youth violence.

These most serious cases are prominent in public concern about the legitimacy and effectiveness of the legal system. They are also difficult but important tests of the general principles that are supposed to be in play throughout the system. Homicide is one important domain to explore when trying to determine the motives and principles that should be at work in other youth crime and delinquency cases. If there is a real gap between what we do and what we say, a close look at decision making in homicide cases will probably reveal it.

This chapter discusses the substantive principles that should govern the punishment of adolescents who kill. The first section shows that the stereotypical versions of juvenile and criminal courts are not well suited to attain just results in adolescent homicides. The second section uses cases reported in the news to explore the multiple varieties of youth homicides. The third section uses the diminished responsibility and room-to-reform conceptions discussed in chapter 5 as a method of exploring punishment principles for adolescent killers. The fourth section sets out specific case studies in the meaning of diminished responsibility: (1) the ages at which homicide offenders should be considered to be partially but not fully responsible, (2) appropriate methods for determining deserved punishments for adolescent killers, (3) constructive homicide liability as a problem for the criminal law of adolescence, and (4) capital punishment for young killers.

A False Dichotomy

If the only choice available for the trial and punishment of adolescent homicide cases was between a juvenile court solely concerned with treatment and a criminal court that ignored the age and circumstances of the defendants, the task of finding appropriate responses would be an impossible one. The intentional taking of life without justification requires a punitive response in most circumstances in which the offender has even a minimal appreciation of the nature of his or her act. Thus punishment must be one of the appropriate responses of any legal authority responsible for addressing adolescent homicide.

But the proper punishment for 15-year-olds who kill must take into account their immaturity and other particular circumstances. Otherwise the legal authority that determines guilt and punishment will not be coherent in making retributive judgments. The popular assumption that trying very young defendants in criminal court removes any necessity to consider their immaturity and other limits is mistaken but revealing. The transfer of juveniles is often described as a decision to "try this defendant as an adult." But if the defendant is 15 years old and of slightly subnormal intelligence, to try and punish him as if he were adult in all respects is a dangerously counterfactual enterprise.

The language used to describe the process of transferring defendants to criminal court is itself an invitation to what psychiatrists call "magical thinking," in which it is imagined that changing the location of a case will suddenly remove the characteristics that cause conflict and ambivalence. The physical reality of jurisdictional transfer is rather mundane—to try an accused as an adult in a criminal court changes only the location of the hearing; it does not change the characteristics of the defendant. If we could in fact transform adolescents into adults by an act of juridical will, the procedure would be in great demand by parents and schools in circumstances far removed from delinquency and crime. This particular branch of magical thinking was immortalized by the revolutionary leader in the Woody Allen film *Bananas,* who proclaims in his inaugural address that "All children under sixteen are hereby sixteen."

The statistics in chapter 7 on waivers from juvenile to criminal courts illustrate the unique problems that are generated by adolescents accused of homicide. The proportion of juvenile homicide charges waived in Texas is six times as large as for the crime with the next highest rate of transfer petitions; and the gap between waiver rates in homicide and those for other offenses is much larger than the contrast between other classes of offenses (Dawson 1992; Eigen 1981a).

The sanctioning options usually available in juvenile court fall short of the perceived need for punishment in a substantial proportion of homicide cases. Pressure for greater punishment can be accommodated either by giving more punishment power to juvenile courts or by transferring defendants to criminal courts, which already have much greater punishment powers. In either case an appropriate judicial performance in adolescent homicides should require a particularized inquiry about the offense and the offender, a mixture of factual detail and principles that has been specifically fashioned from an analysis of homicide offenders and their crimes.

It is therefore discouraging that the processing of thousands of adolescent homicides through state criminal courts has produced very little discussion of the particular deserts of those accountable. This silence is consistent with three different possibilities:

1. The lack of particular analysis of adolescent homicides is an indication that transferred defendants are treated with equal severity as adults.
2. The sentencing discretions available in the prosecution and adjudication procedures result in leniency toward youthful defendants that is substantially without announced principle or discernible pattern.
3. There is a silent common law of unarticulated principles that could be used to both explain and predict the punishment choices.

The most likely of these patterns is probably the second. The system for deciding the punishment of immaturity is probably fundamentally lawless. If so, the lack of appropriate legal standards to explain outcomes in homicide cases would have negative consequences that reach far beyond the particular results. If the outcomes are arbitrary, the pattern of arbitrariness is quite likely to be contagious. If the high stakes in homicide cases cannot produce dialogue and analysis of the justice of particular outcomes, there is little prospect of doing better in the treatment of lesser crimes. To default in providing a principled analysis of the punishment in homicide cases is to run the substantial risk that the whole process will be unprincipled.

Immaturity and Culpability: Some Lessons from Malcolm Shabazz

A New York case that was widely publicized in the summer of 1997 is an instructive illustration of the manifold impact of youth and immaturity on the just punishment for an offense. Malcolm Shabazz was a much traveled 12-year-old when he obtained gasoline and deliberately set a fire in the apartment of his custodial grandmother, knowing that she was at home. Malcolm is the grandson of the black radical Malcolm X, and his grandmother, Betty Shabazz, was Malcolm X's widow. She died as a result of the burns she sustained in the fire.

Testimony at court hearings portrayed Malcolm as extremely troubled, with clinical indications of schizophrenia and a documented history as a chronic fire setter. The boy's defense attorney and a clinical psychologist retained by the prosecution both denied that the defendant intended to kill his grandmother. "I do not believe he consciously meant to do harm to his grandmother," said Dr. Elizabeth Osborn, a clinical psychologist hired by the prosecution. "I believe it was an unconscious act to scare her, make her change, get her to do what he wanted" (Gross 1997).

The youth and immaturity of the offender affect a large number of factors that bear on the just punishment in this case. Data about youth and immaturity may be required to make a judgment about whether the chronic fire-setting behavior was compulsive (a condition not uncommon in this age group), whether the defendant subjectively appreciated the risk of death or of great bodily harm that was attendant on his act, and the plausibility of the defendant's fantasy of an imaginary companion in charge of his decisions (Gross 1997).

What is crystal clear in the Shabazz case is that youth and immaturity are not just factors to be added on to modify an otherwise deserved penalty for a particular course of conduct and its result. The immaturity of an actor has a pervasive influence on a large number of subjective elements of the offense, including cognition, volition, and the appreciation that behavior like setting a fire can produce results like death. The defendant's status and perceptions are relevant to a large number of issues, each of which can affect the extent of personal culpability and therefore of deserved punishment.

To use a metaphor from mathematics, immaturity is not just a single variable in the equation that determines punishment but a characteristic that may affect many different variables. It is best to think of youth and immaturity as factors that may influence every aspect of conduct, other than the character of the resulting harm, that plays a major role in determining the extent of blameworthiness. Malcolm Shabazz and a 25-year-old arsonist with no known developmental difficulties are not two different sorts of people who have committed the same crime; they are two different sorts of people who have committed different crimes, offenses that are fundamentally different because of the characteristics and perceptions of the offenders.

The fatal fire that Malcolm Shabazz set was not the typical act of homicidal youth violence for a number of reasons. He was much younger than the typical juvenile killer. The indications of mental illness are much more substantial than in the usual run of cases. The intention to injure is usually easier to infer because of the use of a gun, knife, or personal force on the deceased. But the potentially pervasive influence of youth and immaturity on the subjective factors that affect the degree of personal culpability is a standard feature of the lethal violence of adolescents.

The Malcolm Shabazz case is not a typical instance of adolescent killing for one other reason: There are no typical cases of adolescent homicide. The substantial variety encountered in adolescent homicide is apparent to any conscientious reader of the daily press. At the opposite end of the spectrum from Malcolm Shabazz is the Lam Choi case, reported in the same month:

> Lam Choi, the alleged slayer of crime boss Cuong Tran, was certified yesterday to stand trial as an adult. . . . Tran, thirty-seven, was shot to death at 1:40 A.M. on November 15 after leaving the Pierce Street Annex, a popular bar at Fillmore and Greenwich Streets. . . . Choi, who was seventeen at the time of the shootings, was allegedly in a group with three adults and another youth the night of Tran's slaying. Prosecutors said the group spoke with the victim inside the bar and four of them followed him to his car, where Choi shot Tran. (Schwartz 1997)

Yet another recent San Francisco Bay shooting, a case in which the victim survived a nearly fatal wound, overlaps very little with either the Shabazz or the Choi circumstances:

Police said children who witnessed the late-morning incident told them that a thirteen-year-old boy deliberately shot the girl after she dared him to use the handgun he was carrying. Witnesses said the two got into a shoving match, the argument escalated and he fired one shot into her chest. (Walker and Herscher 1997)

A further case from the current season's crop of newspaper coverage concerned the sentencing of the young man who, at age 14, fired the shots that killed one British tourist and injured a second in Florida. This defendant was the youngest of the three teens who stopped the car but also the only one of the group who fired a gun (Peltier 1997).

Another adolescent homicide received sustained media coverage just as this text was being prepared for publication. In West Paducah, Kentucky, a 14-year-old high school freshman broke up a high school prayer meeting by opening fire with a .22 caliber handgun. Twelve shots were fired. Two of the students died from the gunshot wounds, and six others were injured (Hoversten 1997).

The assertion that there are no typical adolescent killings is a jurisprudential argument rather than a criminological one. The statistical analysis of homicide cases involving adolescent offenders does reveal recurrent fact patterns, many of which have been discussed in chapters 2 and 3. Overwhelmingly, the weapon used in fatal assaults is the firearm. When homicides are committed by juveniles, there is a much higher likelihood of more than one offender than when homicide is committed by adults. Also, the rate of homicidal injuries is much higher among the two oldest age groups typically within the jurisdiction of the juvenile court: 16- and 17-year-olds.

However, blameworthiness of adolescent killers comes in many different degrees. When it is time to assess an individual defendant's conduct and circumstances to determine the degree of his or her culpability, both the number of significant variables and the distribution of factors that influence culpability are great. There is, first, the age of the accused, as well as the age-related judgment and experience of a particular defendant. Second, there are the precipitating circumstances that led to the lethal assault and the extent to which these were the fault of the accused. If there was a fight, who started it? Who was responsible for the first use of lethal force? If there was group involvement, the extent to which a particular defendant's conduct was responsible for the lethal outcome must be considered. Thus the degree of culpability for homicide will be spread over a wide range, with a relatively small concentration of cases at any particular point on the continuum. If there were ever an attractive group of homicide cases for prix fixe penalties, juvenile killers are certainly not in that category.

The wide range and difficulty in determining the deserved punishment in juvenile killings are also arguments against guideline grids or other mechanically produced sentencing benchmarks, which tend to rely on a very few characteristics, such as age and previous criminal record, to produce modal sentencing values. More appropriate to the complexity of the task would be a common law of adolescent culpability constructed over time in the course of judicial analysis of large numbers of youth homicide cases.

Yet the existing appellate court discussion of juvenile homicide cases involves much of the judicial effort that would be necessary to construct a common law of culpability, with almost none of its benefits. Appellate courts consider the circumstances of adolescent homicide cases in the course of reviewing the propriety of judicial waiver from juvenile court jurisdiction. The best that can be expected from this process is the division of defendants into two rough categories characterized by different average levels of culpability. What cannot be addressed are the principles that should govern an appropriate response to a particular killing, whether it has been adjudicated in a juvenile or a criminal court.

The Theory Gap

Given the high volume of homicide cases and the substantial importance of each offense, the absence of a sustained analysis of culpability is both a peculiar and an important gap. There is a lack of theory concerning the principles that should govern the punishment of adolescent killers. Part of the explanation may be the fact that the issues involved do not all comfortably fit into unified categories of legal theory or court jurisdiction. In the United States, the juvenile court and the criminal court are regarded as not merely two different legal institutions but also two different subjects for analysis and theory. In the Shabazz case, the 12-year-old Malcolm appeared in family court but would have been processed in the criminal courts of New York if he had been 13. The problems in comprehending Malcolm Shabazz's case do not change dramatically on his thirteenth birthday, but as long as we segregate the two systems there is no coordinated way to consider their joint problems.

Another reason for the lack of a theory is the preoccupation with the jurisdictional questions that characterizes policy debates about violent adolescents. Americans conduct long dialogues about what kind of court should try juveniles accused of homicide under the mistaken impression that they are addressing substantive questions about the degree of penal responsibility for these criminal acts.

A Practice in Search of a Theory

The absence of analytic attention to the proper punishment for young homicide defendants does not mean that the present system ignores age and immaturity when deciding on sanctions in juvenile and criminal courts. There is substantial evidence that age and immaturity are powerful influences on practice. Texas prosecutors, it will be recalled, do not even request transfer to criminal court in seven out of every ten homicide charges (see table 7.1). The relatively thin evidence on the youngest offenders in criminal courts also suggests that factors associated with youth produce lesser punishments (Greenwood et al. 1980). The current system in homicide cases seems like a classic case of what has been called "practice in search of a theory" (Vorenberg and Vorenberg 1973). But the combination of high stakes, nonexistent principles, and the low visibility of discretion is a prescription for arbitrariness and injustice. Coherent theory that is specific to adolescent homicide is an important practical need in the justice system, not merely a matter of academic nicety.

Two Principles Applied

This section uses the two broad doctrines in chapter 5 as the organizing categories for policy analysis of adolescents charged with homicide. The first surveys the issues generated by diminished responsibility as a doctrine of substantive criminal law applicable to young killers. The second discusses the ways in which government policies toward children and youths, the sorts of concerns earlier discussed under the heading of room to reform, might affect both the extent of punishment and the conditions under which it should be administered.

Diminished Responsibility and Desert

Those elements of an offender's constitution and perception that are relevant to diminished responsibility should affect the amount of punishment deserved as a consequence of conviction for a particular criminal act. Some theorists would like to have one deserved punishment for a particular offense by a particular offender, the one appropriate penal price for an offense; but I hold with Norval Morris (1977), who considers desert to be a guiding principle, one that defines a range of punishments that are consistent with the degree of blameworthiness in a particular case. Set the punishment below the minimum that is deserved, and the community will suffer because the consequences to the defendant unduly depreciate the seriousness of the criminal act in the circumstances in which it was committed. Set the punishment above the maximum level that is deserved, and both the community and the offender will suffer because more suffering than is justified by the particular circumstances of the offender's culpability will have been imposed. But any punishment within the deserved range would be considered retributively appropriate.

The offender's diminished responsibility should be part of the elements of the offense that define the appropriate range of deserved punishment in that particular case. The immaturity, psychological and perceptual handicaps, and inability to appreciate consequences, which characterize the agreed-upon facts about Malcolm Shabazz, are all important elements that establish a range of just punishments in his case; and these factors would seem to be relevant whether the sentencing court was a juvenile or a criminal tribunal. When elements of diminished responsibility are frequently encountered, they should be incorporated into the basic framework of the minimum and maximum punishments available. If such factors can be used only to guide discretion within a range of minimum punishment decided on other grounds, the calculation will come too late in the process to ensure that the objective of retributive proportionality can be achieved.

Four general observations can be made about diminished responsibility because of youth and the selection of punishment for adolescent killers. First, doctrines of diminished responsibility should be applicable throughout the full spectrum of the severity of an offense. The politically popular notion that immaturity should be allowed to mitigate deserved punishment only in relatively harmless crimes is nonsensical. If subjective culpability is relevant to deserved punishment at all, there is no principled basis on which one can impose a ceiling of seriousness beyond which an offender's lack of maturity or judgment is irrelevant.

Mitigation of punishment because of diminished responsibility may hamper the effectiveness of criminal law as an instrument of control, but if moral consistency is the appropriate standard, diminished responsibility should stand or fall as an issue of general applicability. Homicide should not be excluded from the reach of otherwise applicable doctrines of diminished responsibility.

Second, the greater the significance of subjective rather than objective elements in determining the range of appropriate punishments for a crime, the greater the impact of diminished capacity because of immaturity on deserved punishment. The more the applicable branch of the criminal law concerns itself with not simply harm inflicted but also the circumstances of advertence and intention that produced it, the larger the potential role for personal handicaps that diminish subjective culpability in mitigating the range of deserved punishment.

This emphasis on the subjective makes the criminal law of homicide an area where the potential influence of mitigation is enormous. Criminal acts that cause death are variously classified in the United States as involuntary manslaughter, manslaughter, second degree murder, first degree murder, and (in three-quarters of the states) capital murder. From manslaughter to first degree murder, the range of minimum punishment is from probation to life imprisonment or execution, and the elements that differentiate these crimes are almost exclusively the subjective features of intent, advertence, and motivation that highlight the importance of doctrines of diminished responsibility. When the difference between premeditation (first degree murder) and malice (second degree murder) can mean fifteen years' more imprisonment (Zimring, Eigen, and O'Malley 1976) and when equally lethal acts can be punished by probation (if negligent) or long imprisonment (if grossly reckless), a defendant's youth and immaturity should have a very large influence on the level of deserved punishment.

There are also branches of the substantive criminal law where individual guilt and punishment are determined almost solely by an individual's intent, rather than physical participation in criminal acts, through such doctrines as the liability of conspirators for the criminal acts committed by their coconspirators and the penal liability of an accessory for the crimes of the principal (Kadish 1985). The greater the weight that the law places on the solely subjective dimensions of behavior in a particular case, the greater the mitigational potential of diminished responsibility because of immaturity. When the only basis for punishment is the agreement and intention of the defendant, the defendant's immaturity should have a major impact on the deserved punishment.

The greater leverage of diminished responsibility as an accessory is of tremendous practical significance for adolescent homicide because so many violent acts committed by teenagers are committed in groups. We saw in chapter 2 that the majority of all family court charges for serious crimes in New York involved co-offenders. In the last section of this chapter, we see that half of all offenders under 18 who were arrested for homicide were arrested with at least one other person. When the circumstances that generate a homicide charge involve only the offender's presence or knowledge, rather than physical participation in the infliction of injuries that cause death, the reduction in the range of deserved punishment for the passive, or tag-along, accessories can and should be quite substantial. I return to this point when discussing constructive liability for unintended outcomes.

The high volume of accessorial charges is one important reason why a relatively small proportion of juvenile homicide charges result in prosecutorial requests for judicial waiver. The manifestations of intention of a triggerman in a fatal gun assault are far more substantial than those of the 14-year-old associate standing next to the shooter or the 16-year-old waiting in the car. Also, the link between the defendant's act and the harm inflicted is much closer for the triggerman.

Third, it is important to recognize the substantial number of different blameworthiness issues where the defendant's overall immaturity, inexperience in understanding the link between risk taking and causing harm, and incapacity to control or deflect peer pressure should be taken into account in setting punishment for homicides. In addition to the standard questions regarding mens rea and mistake, the immaturity of an accused might also be relevant to the application of the standard presumptions of Anglo-American law. Recall the prosecution psychologist who believed that Malcolm Shabazz did not intend the death of his grandmother when he started a fire in her apartment. The standard slogan in criminal law is that "a man intends the natural and probable consequences of his actions." Should we be quick to assume that a boy intends the natural and probable consequences of his actions when that boy is 12, or 14, or 16 years of age? A number of standard criminal law doctrines, including strict liability, may not fit the circumstances and psychology of immature defendants as well as they are believed to suit moral judgments about competent adults.

The large number of issues in which an offender's age and immaturity can be relevant to the range of deserved punishment suggests a
procedural consequence that is contrary to the current trend in processing juvenile homicide cases. Case-by-case determinations of culpability by a judge would seem as important in homicide cases as in
any other type of criminal case. Both waiver hearings and individualized sentencing determinations may be necessary to meet the complex challenge of justice in adolescent homicide cases, but the legislative trend is in exactly the opposite direction. The approved
mode for murder charges is transfer at the discretion of the prosecution, and the substantive law that governs sentencing in criminal
courts is utterly silent on immaturity and its implications. The last
section of this chapter concerns some of the many questions of culpability that need to be addressed by criminal courts.

Homicide Sentencing and Youth Policy

One important standard for a justice system is the extent to which it
can adjudicate young offenders without compromising the objectives
of government policy toward young people in general. I argue in
chapter 5 that youths who violate the law are nonetheless the young
people who must be considered subjects of a government youth
policy. The slogan for this conclusion is that the kid is a criminal but
the criminal is still a kid (Greenwood and Zimring 1985). The principal objective of policy in the adjudication and sentencing of minors
is to avoid damaging a young person's development into an adulthood of full potential and free choice; thus the label for this type of
policy is "room to reform."

In an ideal world, the punishment of all young people who violate
the law would avoid disfiguring stigma, debilitating penal confinement, and other permanent developmental handicaps. In an ideal
world, of course, 15-year-olds would not commit intentional homicide. Whenever a community's retributive demands are legitimate
and substantial, there may be a conflict between maximizing the developmental opportunities of young offenders and meeting the retributive necessities of homicide.

One important distinction between concerns of youth policy
and diminished responsibility is that room-to-reform considerations
are outside the range of deserved punishment for a particular individual's participation in a specific criminal act. Every circumstance

that is material to the determination of diminished capacity helps to establish the minimum and maximum deserved punishment. There can thus be no real conflict between diminished capacity and the range of deserved punishments because the former has helped to determine the latter.

But government policy toward youths should not be a part of any kind of equation that determines penal desert. The fact that we want all our teenagers to develop into healthy and realized adults has no direct bearing on the minimum level of punishment felt necessary for an offense or on the maximum beyond which punishment would exceed desert and is therefore unjustified. Also, because the interests of a youth policy are not a part of the determination of desert, the two may be in direct conflict. The smallest punishment appropriate to desert for a terrible crime may inflict exactly the kind of damage that government youth policy seeks to avoid.

When there is unavoidable conflict between the objectives of youth policy and the minimum demands for deserved punishment, the latter should carry the day. This will not be an unjust result if youth and immaturity have been fully accommodated in the calculation of diminished responsibility, but the outcome in such cases will be a disservice to socially important interests by not allowing young people to fully recover from their adolescent mistakes. However, when desert and youth support conflict, electing the minimum punishment becomes the sad necessity of the sentencing court.

Still, youth policy can be much better accommodated, even in the treatment of adolescent killers, than is evident in current practice. The value of promoting normal adolescent development can properly influence the amount of punishment selected within the confines of an already established desert range, and the nature and conditions of adolescent punishment can be designed in ways that will serve the interests of government youth policy vastly better than the current system.

To say that a government policy that favors youth development will not affect the range of punishments deserved by particular young offenders is far from saying that the policy should have no influence on the penalty selected in particular cases. First, the range of deserved penalties for serious crimes is frequently substantial, and the influence of youth policy within that range can make a big difference. To oversimplify, assume that the range of deserved punishment for a particular type of involvement in homicide is two and one-half years at the minimum and nine years at the maximum. Even youth policies that do not have an impact on those minimum and maximum values can be powerful determinants of the actual sentence.

Second, youth policy can influence the form of a criminal punishment within a range that is established by other considerations. A recurrent example is the greater use of indeterminacy in the sentencing of young offenders convicted of very serious offenses. The presumed malleability of young offenders and the likelihood that fundamental changes in character and maturity will occur in the course of penal confinement have resulted in an emphasis on indeterminacy in the sentencing of older youths in criminal courts. Both the Federal Youth Corrections Act, which was a sentencing option in the United States until 1984, and parallel provisions in Great Britain and on the continent of Europe reflected this emphasis. All of these provisions were established for the criminal court sentencing of young offenders. In that sort of system, the effective minimum for the young offender will be the bottom of the range of deserved punishment, but the substantive concerns of a youth policy might produce the offender's release "at the pleasure of Her Majesty" shortly after that minimum has been met.

The other way in which policy toward children and youths should influence the treatment of young homicide offenders is atrociously ignored in much American practice. No matter how serious the crime committed by a 14-year-old, there is no reason short of magical thinking for concluding that the young offender has become an adult in matters such as the need for education and vulnerability to adult predation. I would argue that whenever a young offender's need for protection, education, and skill development can be accommodated without frustrating community security, there is a government obligation to do so.

One of two sentiments seems to underlie the frequent assertion that young persons who commit serious crimes do not require the services and schooling usually appropriate to their age. The first notion is that truly serious crime is a mark of maturity, a benchmark that indicates that legal emancipation is appropriate. This inference has never been backed by any empirical data. It seems instead to follow as the obverse of an assumption that the truly immature are incapable of committing homicide. The second sentiment is that withdrawal of all special projections is an appropriate punishment for crime. Some proponents of adult penalties would extend treating youths as if they were adults to denial of special conditions of confinement such as age segregation and protection from older prisoners, educational programs, counseling, and special mental health services. The implicit argument is that young offenders do not deserve anything that might benefit them, as youth-oriented protections might.

But as long as the security of confinement is not compromised, it is difficult to see a genuine conflict between providing youth services and punishing even the most serious offenses. On utilitarian grounds, the education and training of the young is a positive value even if long-term confinement is its context. From a retributive perspective, the provision of age-appropriate conditions of confinement would seem analogous to providing needed medical care for all prisoners, a continuing obligation that does not compromise the punitive bite of confinement. Education and security from predatory assault are not privileges conferred on young persons and revokable as a consequence of misbehavior.

To summarize: The interaction of youth policy with the retributive necessity of punishment is a contingent one. When the community's minimum level of required punishment is too high to accommodate full protection of the development of the young offender, there will be a direct conflict between what is desirable for all adolescents and what can be provided for the most serious adolescent offenders. For such true conflicts, the need for minimum deserved punishment will control.

Often, however, there will be opportunities to find punishment within the desert range that allows the offender's growth and development into near normal adulthood, and it will always be possible to provide education and age-appropriate security and conditions of confinement to even the most culpable of adolescent killers. In these cases, there is no good reason to terminate special policies toward youths that do not conflict with the demands of penal justice.

Case Studies in Diminished Culpability

This section is a modest down payment on the substantial work that will be necessary if the implications and limits of responsibility in youth violence are appropriately developed. I discuss here four sub-

stantive issues that range from age boundaries for diminished capacity to potential eligibility for capital punishment.

The Age Span of Diminished Responsibility

A substantial number of practical questions stand between the principles discussed earlier and an operating system of adjudication and
disposition of adolescent homicide. One question concerns the age
boundaries of diminished responsibility. At the lower extreme, when
should we declare the transition from incapacity to minimum states
of capacity not inconsistent with some punishment for serious
crime? The common law had a conclusive presumption of incapacity
below age 7, and presumed capacity after age 14.

Figure 8.1 shows the distribution of all homicide arrests for
offenders under the age of 18 for 1995. Homicide arrests are rare
events under age 13 and infrequent under age 15. More 15-year-olds
are arrested for homicide than the total of all ages under 15, and
more 16-year-olds are arrested for homicide than the total of all ages
under 16.

Figure 8.2 shows estimated rates of homicide charges in juvenile
court by the age at referral. Age 13 has a very low rate of prosecution
referral. Significant homicide-charging activity begins at age 14 and
increases steadily thereafter. By age 17, the charging rate is nineteen
times as large as at age 13. In practice, the significant threshold for
the minimum ages for homicide prosecution are 12 through 14. It is
not clear whether discretionary arrest and charging play a major role
in the near zero rates below age 14. The border between incapacity
and capacity is usually regarded as a matter of case-by-case determination, in the first instance by prosecutors and in the second by juvenile court judges.

After the age of minimum culpability is attained, how long should
diminished capacity play a role in determining deserved punishment, and how great a role should it play? The correct policy answer
to this question depends on the range of capacities believed relevant
to culpability and the ages at which they are typically attained. If all
the characteristics of diminished responsibility outlined in chapter 5
are relevant to punishment, inquiry about such matters could extend
up to and not infrequently beyond age 18 in homicide cases. If the
lack of experience in learning to deflect peer pressure and in dealing
with provocation are regarded as mitigating elements, most adolescent offenders will be operating at far from trivial deficits. In con-

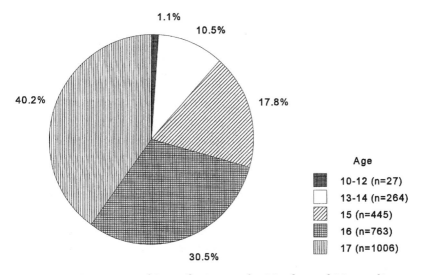

Figure 8.1. Percentage of Juvenile Arrests for Murder and Nonnegligent Manslaughter, Ages 10–17, 1995. Source: U.S. Department of Justice, Federal Bureau of Investigation (1995).

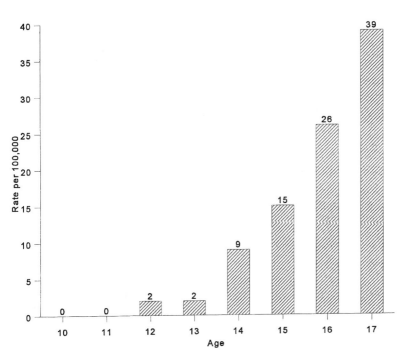

Figure 8.2. Estimated Rates per 100,000 of Prosecution of Youths, 1992. Source: Snyder and Sickmund (1995).

trast, most of the basic capacities for moral judgments are achieved earlier, normally by age 14 or 15. The greater the emphasis on experience and social skills, the larger the degree of social and experiential development that must occur before criminal acts can be said to deserve the full measure of punishment.

These general observations fall far short of a specific schedule of degrees of responsibility linked to age or other attributes of the offender. One reason for this is the absence of good data on the social skills and social experience of adolescent offenders. The important elements of penal maturity have yet to be agreed upon, let alone assessed in large numbers of cases. There is reason to believe that concentrated efforts will tell us much more than we now know about the social psychology of adolescent violence, and this knowledge about general patterns of development will be helpful to some extent in developing policy.

But I doubt whether even advanced knowledge of adolescent development and the particular characteristics of young violent offenders will produce a satisfactory schedule of punishments normed to age or prior offenses. The range of individual variation among youths of the same age is notoriously large. The relationship of a particular young offender to the criminal harm is another important dimension, and this will interact with different ages in different ways. The significant variables in determining the proper punishment for a teen killer will not fit comfortably into a two-dimensional sentencing grid. For such cases, I know of no superior alternative to the combination of wide potential sentencing frames, individual judicial judgments with reasons, and appellate review.

This lack of fit with price-list sentencing is a special characteristic of adolescent homicide cases for two related reasons. First, the degree to which subjective elements influence deserved punishment is great in homicide cases of all kinds, so a wide range of punishments should be available even before immaturity complicates the matter. Second, price-list sentencing works best when the major influence in the appropriate sentence is the type of offense committed rather than variations in the offender's subjective state or capacity to control behavior. If most burglaries are punished within a relatively narrow range for offenders with equivalent criminal records, the sentencing guideline can be relatively specific and not unjust. The less important the particular offense is in defining the specific sentence, the less useful the sentencing guideline system that selects offense as the basic organizing category.

The Calculus of Juvenile Desert

Once the substantive decision is made to recognize immaturity as a mitigation of culpability and thus an influence on the range of deserved punishment, two different approaches can determine appropriate sanctions for particular young offenders—discounting and independent determination. In a discounting strategy, the starting point for a calculation of the deserved punishment for a youth would be the deserved punishment of an adult for the same type of offense. If adult burglars with particular criminal histories typically get four years of penal confinement at sentencing, the way to calculate the appropriate penalty for a 15-year-old burglar is to determine a discount from that sentence. If, on the average, conditions of diminished responsibility for 15-year-olds should produce a 50 percent punishment reduction, one calculates the punishment for the youth by multiplying the adult sentence times 1.0 minus the discount, or in this case, 4 years $\times$ (1.0 − 0.5) = 2 years. Variations on this discounting strategy, which is directly dependant on the adult penalty for the type of punishment and its duration, have been suggested for juveniles in criminal courts (Feld 1998) and in juvenile courts (Institute for Judicial Administration 1977).

Little has been written about how the wide variety of different characteristics of adolescent offenders might be translated into a schedule of discounts. Barry Feld (1988), who advocates discounting for young offenders in criminal court as an alternative to the current juvenile court system, describes the process:

> This categorical approach might take the form of an explicit "youth discount" at sentencing. A fourteen-year-old offender would receive, for example, 25 percent of the adult penalty, a sixteen-year-old defendant, 50 percent, and an eighteen-year-old adult the full penalty, as is presently the case. The "deeper discounts" for younger offenders correspond to the developmental continuum of responsibility.

The notion is evidently for the same age-based discounts across all categories of offense types and liability.

A contrasting approach might take its hierarchy of offense seriousness from the adult system, so that burglary would be regarded as less serious than robbery but more serious than theft, but would not use the average penal sanctions imposed on adults as the basis for computing the penalties for adolescents. For a number of reasons, I believe that such independent determinations of sanctions for young offenders are more appropriate in both juvenile and criminal courts.

The independent calculation of sanctions for young homicide offenders more accurately reflects both the nonquantifiable nature of criminal punishments and the large variation in levels of culpability that characterize adolescent offenders. The average term of penal confinement for adult killers is generally an aggregate of many different grades of offenses and degrees of criminal culpability. Time served for voluntary manslaughter may be not much longer than time served for nonfatal violent crimes. Second degree murder sentences are much longer in many jurisdictions. Aggregating the two groups of sentences and taking a group mean would provide a rather arbitrary measure of desert for adult killers. Providing separate averages for the two offense categories assumes that the types of homicides reflected in the adult distribution are also found among juveniles and that the relationship of blameworthiness in the two classes is the same for juveniles as it is for adults. This does not seem to me a plausible set of assumptions.

There is also no reason to suppose that terms of penal confinement proportionally express different levels of deserved condemnation. Is the community condemnation expressed in a ten-year sentence twice as much as in a five-year sentence, and is five years five times one year? If not, discounting should not be based on a fixed proportion of a term of confinement. If adult punishments are inexact, even crude measures of blameworthiness and variations in terms of confinement are only roughly correlated with levels of culpability, providing a specified fraction of an adult penalty as a youth penalty or creating a schedule of different fractions treats a crude and multiply determined average of prison time served as if it were a much more sensitive and accurate measure of the community's sense of deserved punishment. No matter how carefully the fractions are measured and reported, the enormous margin of error to be found cannot be reduced. Indeed, it turns out that any system of discounting fractions for young offenders may exacerbate the problems that result from the problematic nature of adult penalties as a currency of culpability.

First, age is an incomplete proxy for levels of maturity during the years from age 12 to 18. The variation among individuals of the same age is great, and individualized determinations of immaturity are thus superior to averages based on aggregate patterns (Zimring 1982: 126–132). Second, the vulnerabilities associated with early and middle adolescence play a more important part in explaining some patterns of homicide than others. The passive accomplice who acquiesces in a robbery that turns lethal rather than be called chicken by his peers is a more attractive candidate for extensive mitigation of punishment than one of the same age who instigated the robbery, even though that more active role was also motivated by the need to make a positive social impression. Some types of provocation in group conflicts may also lead to extensive mitigation, as when the 13-year-old in Oakland was accused of being "too chicken" to shoot by his victim. Those situations that put extreme pressure on particular vulnerabilities characteristic of adolescents make them strong candidates for sharply reduced punishment when a fatality results. Moreover, the large variation in the level of achieved maturity interacts with the differential vulnerabilities found in different circumstances to present a complicated landscape, one much too complex for an age-determined series of presumed discounts from a standing price list of penalties.

My own view is that measuring mitigated penalties as a percentage of usual time served would be an inappropriate strategy in both juvenile and criminal courts. In juvenile courts, the expected sentence for an adult guilty of a similar offense may be only remotely related to the proper disposition of the youthful offender. The type of confinement to be served is different, the adolescent and the adult have different senses of time, and the mix of purposes behind sanctioning decisions is also not the same as in the criminal court.

The case for fixed discounts might seem stronger for young offenders being sentenced in criminal courts but is still far from compelling. The criminal law has extensive experience in creating offense categories to allow mitigated punishment for homicides. Second degree murder was invented as one such mitigation strategy; voluntary manslaughter is another. It is worth noting that nowhere was the penalty for manslaughter derived as a fraction of the penalty for first degree murder. Each step down the ladder of culpability for homicide has its own penalty range, which has never in my experience been derived as a fraction of the going rate for particular grades of murder.

The traditional method of special sentences for youths in criminal courts also avoided deriving punishments by using a particular fraction of adult penalties in the United States or in Europe. Instead, indeterminate terms with relatively short minimum sentences is a typical pattern. The fact that fixed discounts have never been adopted as the mechanism to implement diminished responsibility should inspire caution.

Constructive Doctrine and Adolescent Homicide Liability

A cluster of related doctrines imposes criminal liability on adults for the lethal acts of others and for deaths that they might cause, even if a particular defendant did not have a specific intent to injure. These include the felony murder rules, the doctrine of accessorial liability, and rules stating that accessories are guilty of the criminal acts committed by those they have aided or agreed to aid in the commission of a crime. A standard example of the web of constructive liability begins when A, B, and C agree to rob a convenience store. A provides the plans, but stays home; B drives C to the store but waits in the car; C pulls a gun on the salesclerk, who resists. The gun goes off during the struggle and the salesclerk is mortally wounded. A, B, and C are all guilty of first degree murder in most U.S. states. The rules of accessorial liability make A and B liable for C's acts in furtherance of their common design. The felony murder rules make the intention to further the robbery a sufficient mental state to generate liability for first degree murder if the robbery causes a death. The intention to commit the robbery is the legal equivalent of malice, and murder statutes typically impose first degree liability on all parties accountable for the forcible felony that caused the death (Zimring and Zuehl 1986).

Rules relating to accessorial liability are of great importance to adolescent offenders because group involvement is greater in teen violence than at any other age. Our analysis of Federal Bureau of Investigation homicide data shows that just over half of all persons arrested for homicide under the age of 18 were involved in an offense for which at least one other homicide arrest was made. That is more than twice the proportion of multiple arrest defendants in over-18 homicide arrests, or 51 percent versus 23 percent (U.S. Department of Justice, Federal Bureau of Investigation 1994). Felony murder doctrine is also important—about one-fifth of all homicide arrests of persons under 18 are for police-nominated felony killings.

Accessorial liability can interact with the vulnerability of adolescents to group pressure to create very marginal conditions for extensive criminal sanctions. This is not to deny that some juvenile accomplices may have played dominant roles in particular deaths. Rather, I would argue that the range of culpability is very great and that the culpability at the low end of the distribution should be rather small. A case can be made for allowing the waiver of a youth to criminal court on solely accessorial responsibility for a killing only if there is evidence that the particular defendant knew of and encouraged the use of lethal force. In a justice system in which only homicide leads to transfer in large proportions, requiring more than constructive liability for homicide would seem to make sense.

I know of no extensive analysis of felony murders and accessorial liability for adolescent offenders. But perhaps large numbers of accused accessories transferred into the criminal courts might lead to the first sustained dialogue about deserved punishment and adolescent accessories in the history of Anglo-American criminal law.

The case for substantial mitigation from accessorial responsibility for a killing is based on the greater emphasis on subjective culpability for the accomplice. The felony murder rule might be distinguishable from other accessory situations. Because it imposes strict liability, no subjective mental state beyond the intention to commit a forcible felony is required, and even 16-year-olds can intend to rob. It might be argued, however, that the law assumes maturity and capacity beyond ordinary adolescent attainments as the foundation on which strict liability for the outcome of forcible felonies is based. The question is not one that has received any sustained attention during a period when most adolescent homicides were disposed of in low-stakes and informal juvenile court hearings, but it would be possible for a court to find that the imposition of strict liability depends on more than minimal capacity for criminal liability in general.

As a practical matter, if transfer to criminal court is to be restricted to cases that are the moral equivalent of intentional homicide, it should not be based solely on liability for the homicidal acts of another under the felony murder rules. This type of restriction would not eliminate criminal court processing of felony killings, but it would restrict the defendants to those whose active support and participation in the killing can be established. The system's most serious sanctions should be reserved for those young offenders whose participation in homicide was not solely as a nonaggressive accomplice. Strict liability to murder prosecution, if retained for any cases, should be reserved for more experienced felons.

Capital Punishment and the Adolescent Killer

The only legal issue concerning the diminished capacity of adolescent killers that has received sustained attention in the United States is the constitutional question of whether the Eighth Amendment's prohibition of cruel and unusual punishment implies that very young killers cannot be executed. Defense attorneys had sought a per se exclusion of persons under 18 at the time an offense was committed from eligibility for the death penalty, arguing from minimum ages that are observed in other nations and in several U.S. states. The U.S. Supreme Court declined that invitation but has excluded the eventual execution of offenders under 16 at the time the crime was committed on Eighth Amendment grounds, even if they are otherwise competent and culpable.

The reasoning of the justices in cases like *Eddings v. Oklahoma* and *Thompson v. Oklahoma* does not provide clear exposition on questions of diminished responsibility for adolescent killers for three reasons. First, the issue comes up in a death penalty context, and strong categorical sentiments about capital punishment dominate the responses of many observers to detailed questions about death penalty policy. To put great weight on the importance of a defendant's youth after *Thompson v. Oklahoma*, it is first necessary to remove the principles to be found in the cases from the death penalty context. This has not yet been done.

Second, the Eighth Amendment cases have a limited basis for constitutional review. It is not the self-appointed duty of the Supreme Court to state a minimum age for execution that would be appropriate on policy grounds. Instead, the Court will only limit state power when clear violations of contemporary standards of decency would otherwise occur. Thus the standards the Court has established may well be far short of the appropriate policy on minimum age that many of the justices might choose as policy.

Third, the Supreme Court emphasized the practices in various punishment systems rather than the reasons behind them. *Thompson v. Oklahoma,* for example, debates how many states have implicit or explicit minimum ages for the death penalty instead of why minimum ages might be regarded as necessary to a morally coherent death penalty. The illumination this provides on basic issues about adolescent capacity and culpability is indirect at best. Diminished responsibility may be the reason for minimum age standards in states and nations that observe age limits for the death penalty, but it is the age limits rather than the rationale for them that has center stage in the constitutional debate.

With these considerable limits, the death penalty case law still has value as a precedent in any discussion of a defendant's youth as a mitigating factor. The four-judge plurality in *Thompson v. Oklahoma* endorsed a prohibition on death for all offenders under the age of 16, and Sandra Day O'Conner's concurrence supported that result in the circumstances of the Oklahoma statute. If the constitution forbids executing anyone for any crime committed before age 16, this must be because a presumption of diminished capacity requires such minimum age standards under the Eighth Amendment. When age at the time of the offense is the standard, the substantive context being enforced must be a notion of diminished culpability for the crime rather than incapacity to comprehend the punishment.

If one reads *Thompson* as suggesting a ban on executions for crimes committed under the age of 16, the use of that limit for the Eighth Amendment rule should not be regarded as an endorsement for the execution of 16- and 17-year-olds who commit murder. The Court has clearly indicated that juries must be instructed that youth beyond the sixteenth birthday can be taken into account in the penalty trial (*Thompson v. Oklahoma*). Also, if *Thompson* is a per se rule for under 16, it is the only instance in death penalty jurisprudence in which a defendant responsible for a capital murder cannot be executed because of diminished capacity at the time of the crime.

Even though the standards for the Eighth Amendment are quite loose, the peculiar facts of capital punishment in the United States could well support an extension of proportionality limits to the seventeenth or eighteenth birthday. With less than 1 execution for every 200 killings, only the most blameworthy of killers should be selected for a capital sanction. On what facts would a 16- or 17-year-old killer be found in the top 1 percent of heinous crimes? Although it might be awkward for a federal court to restrain death sentences for the young because of the distribution of death sentences in other cases, a proportionality review in state court can and should measure the sentences issued to adolescents against the real politics of sentences and execution in a particular jurisdiction.

The struggle in the Supreme Court over death as a sanction for young killers has its broadest impact by establishing general principles to govern the sentencing of young offenders in criminal court. Cases like *Eddings* and *Thompson* involve defendants already waived from juvenile court and convicted of aggravated murder in criminal courts. By restricting the availability of the death sentence, the Court has already recognized that the defendant's youthful status follows him or her into criminal court and precludes the treatment of any young person in criminal court jurisdiction as fully adult for all purposes. The view that young persons are no longer young when transferred to criminal court is not only irrational but also against the weight of U.S. Supreme Court authority. The principle was invoked in Eighth Amendment jurisprudence because of the special status of the death penalty. But the Court's emphasis on the fact of youth rather than on the form of the court is a principle of general applicability.

Conclusion

The search for appropriate legal standards for adolescent homicides is important in its own right and also as an example of the type of analysis that is necessary to determine just punishments for other types of adolescent offenders in criminal courts. Very little legal analysis or argument currently addresses the punishment of serious adolescent offenses in criminal court. This chapter demonstrates the variety and complexity of the issues when the substantive criminal law of homicide is measured against the circumstances and developmental limits usually found in adolescent homicide cases.

The conventional belief about punishment for young killers is that the important decisions have been made once the issue of transfer to criminal court has been decided. Not so. Rather than being the end of difficult decisions, the transfer determination should be regarded as requiring a series of factual and legal inquiries as subtle, problematic, and controversial as can be found in the modern criminal law of personal violence.

Building principle into the punishment of adolescent homicides in criminal courts has been, for some time, an unmet challenge for American criminal law. The increase in automatic transfers and the high priority of youth violence in penal policy remind us that a void in principles at the heart of the legal response to homicide becomes a greater embarrassment with each passing day.

Part III

TWO LARGER CONTEXTS

The first two parts of this book concern the specific nature of American youth violence in the 1990s and the legal doctrines and procedures that have been proposed to respond to it. This concluding section considers some of the ways in which concern about adolescent violence has implications for broader social and legal policies. Chapter 9 addresses the relationship between current worries about youth violence and proposals to change the delinquency jurisdiction of the juvenile courts in the United States. Youth violence has been an important topic for law reform in juvenile justice. It has also been an important symbol for those who wish to change the structure and mission of the American juvenile court. The chapter analyzes the basis for violence-oriented reform in juvenile justice and some specific changes that have been made to adjudicate violent acts in juvenile courts.

The last chapter examines the effect of concerns of the 1990s on American attitudes toward youth and on the policies that public attitudes are likely to support. What does it mean when the only dimensions of a future youth population being considered in Congress are violent crime rates in the year 2010? What characteristics of the current age have contributed to this distorted and dangerous single-issue perspective? What appropriate remedies are available? Among the many casualties of the current war on juvenile violence has been a sense of historical and generational perspective about the problems and prospects of growing up in the United States. I argue that the current crop of fearful projections about future youth populations is based on a dangerous innocence that should never again be permitted to distort the way in which Americans view children and youths.

Youth Violence and the Future of the Juvenile Court

As chapter 1 reported, youth violence has dominated legislative debate and activity concerning juvenile justice throughout the 1990s. This chapter explores the consequences of that domination on the principles and processes of the juvenile court in the United States and on the types of future reform currently being discussed. This chapter considers the broad question of how concern about youth violence may modify the processes and prospects of the juvenile court in its entire delinquency jurisdiction. After a century of development, the juvenile court now operates in the shadow of intense concern about adolescent violence. This chapter addresses the implications of that shadow for the theory and practice of juvenile justice.

The analysis proceeds in four parts. The first distinguishes between youth violence as a specific subject of law reform and youth violence as a symbol that animates broad proposals for change in the character of the juvenile court. The second part examines a possible conflict between the general assumptions of juvenile justice and some categories of young violent offenders. The third part examines changes in the powers and procedures of juvenile courts that have been instituted to cope more effectively with serious offenses of violence. The fourth part considers the particular dangers that are associated with using serious offenses of violence as paradigm cases for the general reform of juvenile justice.

The Violent Juvenile as Subject and Symbol

There is no doubt that debate about the violent juvenile offender has dominated discourse about juvenile justice throughout the 1990s. But a closer look at both the rhetoric and the legislation of recent years suggests that there are two separate processes under way in which public attitudes about violent young offenders are of great importance. The first debate is about the violent juvenile offender as the *subject* of legal change. The 15-year-old with a gun is the image that dominates a discussion about what to do with youths who carry guns or shoot people. The policy at issue is specific to those juveniles who commit offenses that threaten the physical security of others, that is, only to the most serious forms of juvenile violence. The question is whether and when special polices about violence should replace an unchanged general framework of responses by the justice system to juvenile delinquency.

The second policy debate involves the use of the violent juvenile as the *symbol* that justifies the reorientation of the legal system toward young offenders in general, if not toward an even broader segment of the youth population. The Virginia Governor's Commission on Juvenile Justice (1995), mentioned in chapter 1, seems to be using the fear of youth violence to justify changing the entire system. The rhetoric of the commission is not directed toward separating one subsegment of juvenile offenders from others for special treatment. Instead, the distinction is between the benign delinquents of yesteryear, epitomized by "vandalism and childish pranks," and the malignant and dangerous juveniles of the current day, epitomized by "crimes such as murder, rape, and robbery" (p. 3). When the violent juvenile is used as a poster child, meant to represent the general run of young offenders, it is not useful to ask what aspects of violent acts or of offenders are significant in setting these cases apart from the general run of delinquency because the implicit theory of the appeal is that the threatening characteristics of the seriously violent juvenile are broadly shared by other juvenile offenders.

The policy implications of these two versions differ in fundamental ways. To view the seriously violent juvenile as a special policy problem would seem to require the creation of separate principles and processes from those of standard juvenile justice. To use the seriously violent juvenile as the symbol of the contemporary delinquent would call for a reorientation of the entire system.

There would also seem to be conflict between the factual premises that animate the view of the violent juvenile as a separate and discrete problem and the view of the violent juvenile as the delinquent archetype of the current generation. Thus it might seem that these contrasting positions offer the citizen a choice between mutually exclusive theories about young offenders in the 1990s.

In fact, however, the fear of juvenile violence has been used simultaneously to create separate tracks into the criminal court, or blended jurisdiction, and to create a more punitive, less protective juvenile court for all accused delinquents. Even the empirical characterizations of violence seem ambiguous, if not ambidextrous, in terms of whether seriously violent juveniles are representative of their peers. The "juvenile superpredator" of current Washington sound bites certainly seems to be a breed apart from the standard delinquent of this or any other age. Yet talk of 270,000 extra of such superpredators warns us of an entire generation of unprecedented problems that are flooding the courts and correctional systems of American juvenile justice. In legislation, such as the House-passed Federal Juvenile Justice Act of 1997, inconsistent images of the violent youth offender are used to justify both separate processes for violent youths and more punitive policies toward most delinquents. But the inconsistency has yet to be noted.

Youth Violence and the Criteria for Juvenile Court Jurisdiction

The arguments made by those who use the violent juvenile offender as a symbol of the general failure of juvenile justice need not distinguish between violent and other delinquent youths. The position of these critics is that the traditional juvenile court is the wrong place to adjudicate any serious crime committed by teenagers. This is a critique of American juvenile justice rather than an argument based on the particularity of violent crimes or the adolescents who commit them.

But those who wish to retain the traditional features of juvenile court for most 13- to 17-year-olds accused of felonies but exclude either some or all violent offenders must offer distinctions between them. This demands an explicit theory of the kind of case and the kind of young offender that the juvenile court should retain and treat in traditional fashion. For this reason, any detailed argument for the exclusion of some types of violence from juvenile court is noteworthy for what it tells us about the proper role of the juvenile court in general. Also for this reason, a capsule history of the modern juvenile court is necessary as a background to this discussion.

The original theory of juvenile justice was that all minors in need of treatment, including delinquent minors, should receive help in proportion to their needs (Zimring 1982:Chap. 3). Since punishment was not intended, proportionality was not an issue. The only minors who were not to be treated in this way were those not amenable to treatment. Early on, however, serious offenses and repeat offenses were considered strong evidence that the accused delinquent was not amenable and therefore should be expelled from the juvenile court (Twentieth Century Fund 1978).

In its early years, the juvenile court was known for treating minor and relatively serious offenses in similar ways. Reformers' criticism and the introduction of defense lawyers and prosecutors into the system in the 1960s soon resulted in a more important role for the seriousness of the offense in decisions about sanctions and waiver to adult courts. The language of amenability to treatment remained, but particularly serious crimes were associated with waiver and minor status offenses such as truancy were removed as a basis for secure confinement. By the 1980s, proportionality had become a widely accepted standard for judging the fairness of juvenile court dispositions. Both statutes and court cases used seriousness of the offense as a basis for deciding the fitness of an accused for juvenile court jurisdiction.

This idea, however, did not displace either the treatment ideology of the juvenile court or the traditional notion that youth itself and the crimes characteristic of early adolescence should be handled in a separate court. The juvenile court has instead spent a generation as a hybrid institution. The list of factors that determined the suitability of a young offender for juvenile court lengthened with each new turn in the courts' orientation, but the old ideologies were also retained. By the time *Kent v. United States* was decided in the U.S. Supreme Court, the courts were told to consider eight factors in deciding whether an accused delinquent was to be waived to criminal court (*Kent v. United States,* 383 U.S. 541, 1966). In the next twenty years, increasing emphasis was put on the seriousness of the charge, but none of the traditional considerations have been rejected by courts as irrelevant when individual determinations of suitability need to be made.

The list of factors for waiver is an indication of the general principles of juvenile justice. The subject of this section is not individual waiver decisions but rather the issue of whether general statements can be made about the fit between the mission of the juvenile court and violent offenders and violent offenses. My reference to discussions of suitability and amenability in waiver cases is for the purpose of listing the significant characteristics that make a case an attractive

candidate for juvenile court. The effort here is to extract from cases
and literature a list of the criteria of fitness and to then profile what is
known about the distribution of juveniles arrested for violence based
on these characteristics.

Table 9.1 approaches this task by juxtaposing terms that usually
describe fit subjects for juvenile justice with their opposites. The list
of characteristics is a relatively complete one, but the cost of complete coverage is a very substantial overlapping between concepts
and categories. Amenability to treatment, for example, seems closely
related to accepting help and supervision, and most youths who are
changeable would for that reason probably not be strongly committed to criminal values. Nonetheless, each of the eight attributes does
represent different points of emphasis in the evolution of the suitability of offenders for adjudication in juvenile court. What follows
is a brief description of each dimension of suitability, as well as my
assessment of the existing evidence about the distribution of such attributes among adolescents arrested for violent crimes.

The general conclusion is an unsurprising one: The characteristics
of juveniles who commit violent acts are so widely distributed that
the only safe general statement is that categorical generalization
about violent offenders or even those who commit serious acts of
violence is quite difficult. The violent juvenile offender is not a phe-
notype (see Hawkins 1960).

The great grandfather of attributes favorable to jurisdiction by the
juvenile court is amenability to treatment. Because the court was

Table 9.1. Common Descriptions of Favorable Offender Attributes for Juvenile
Court Delinquency Processing and Their Opposites

Favorable	Unfavorable
Amenable to treatment	Not amenable to treatment
Immature	Fully developed, mature
Not committed to criminal values	Committed to criminal values
Changeable	Fixed propensities
Accepts help and supervision	Rejects direction and assistance
Offense typical for developmental phase	Offense not typical for young offender
Responsible for very serious crime	Not responsible for large social cost
Nondangerous	Dangerous

originally organized around a variety of treatment interventions, the more likely a youth is to respond favorably to treatment, the better a prospect he or she is for juvenile court. The absence of amenability to treatment portends the failure of the court's primary mechanism of rehabilitation. Thus, nonresponsive subjects are less suited to juvenile adjudication and threaten the mission of the court.

The amenability to treatment of various subgroups of violent offenders has been the subject of some research over the past few decades. Its focus, however, was on finding specific treatment programs that demonstrated above-average effectiveness. No categorical findings of either high or low amenability to treatment have been issued for entire subclasses of violent offenders. Indeed, generalizations that sweeping are not regarded as attractive subjects for serious empirical research. But the absence of valid generalizations gives us a finding of some importance to the policy process. Since category-wide generalizations are not valid, no general policy toward violent offenders can be justified on amenability grounds.

Immaturity is an obvious hallmark for an institution that regards itself as a court for children. To the extent that immaturity is a plausible explanation for an offender's criminal behavior, we are more likely to embrace juvenile court as a place where the penal consequences can be mitigated because of diminished responsibility. That the immature are still in an unfinished and transitional stage justifies special consideration and special sanctions. The fully mature offender, in contrast, would also seem to be fully responsible and for this reason an attractive prospect for the criminal court and unmitigated punishment.

Very little is known about the level of maturity of violent juveniles. The more serious acts of violence are concentrated in the oldest age categories of the juvenile court—age 16 and 17 years in a court system with a jurisdictional boundary of the eighteenth birthday. The average violent juvenile offender should be somewhat older than juvenile offenders in general. There are, however, no indications that violent juveniles are either more or less mature than other youths of the same age who are arrested. Since arrests for violent crime are now distributed broadly from age 13 on, the actual chronological age of particular subjects would be a much better general indication of immaturity-maturity than the category of offense for which they have been apprehended.

The values and loyalties of young offenders have long been thought especially important by the architects and personnel of

American juvenile courts. A lack of commitment to antisocial values is regarded as a major advantage for the adjudication and treatment of an accused in the juvenile court system. A firm commitment to antisocial values is considered a bad sign, one important dimension of not being amenable to treatment. This raises the issue of whether participation in violence is evidence of substantial commitment to criminal values? It is alleged that some types of violent conduct indicate a strong embrace of a criminal code. Gang violence is the prototypical case, and the image of the gang-banger as a life course persistent criminal type is frequently encountered in the policy debates of the 1990s.

There are two problems in accepting that image, however. First, juvenile gang crime does not correspond in reality to the public perception of drug-trafficking gangs, drug wars, and related violence (Howell 1996). Gang violence is mainly related to turf issues and trivial interpersonal conflicts with other gangs (Decker 1996). Groups and group conflict are hallmarks of adolescent violence (Warr 1996), but they are usually unrelated to the kind of street gang hierarchy that is associated with the image of long-term criminal commitment. Second, even within formal gang structures there are many youths who are transient and peripheral participants without any deep commitment to any value system. Adolescents who join gangs in cities like Denver, Rochester (New York), and Seattle stay in the gang only about one year (see Howell 1998), particularly when gangs are territorial. In a territorial gang, individuals' compliance with gang commands may tell you a great deal more about their address than about their values. For example, Esbensen, Huizinga, and Weiher (1993) found no differences in the extent to which Denver gang members, nongang street offenders, and nonoffenders were involved in eight different conventional activities: holding school-year and summer jobs; attending school; and participating in school athletics, school activities, community athletics, community activities, and religious activities.

Adolescence is a period of human development that is notorious for the tendency to change quickly. Although it may not always be an unqualified benefit to adolescents or to the people around them, the fact that young offenders are subject to quick changes in the pattern of their behavior and their outlook is a positive sign for the legal process. This dynamic quality makes it less likely that patterns of deviance will become ingrained and inevitably be repeated. Because the adolescent is changeable, his or her previous criminal activity is less predictive of future criminal activity; and this general propensity for change may be a good deal broader than amenability to treatment programs. Changeability is the hallmark of a personality system still in the process of formation. In contrast, an offender's fixed propensity to repeat patterns of criminal behavior is bad news for a criminal justice system—and not simply because it is an indication of nonamenability to treatment. The more or less spontaneous patterns of desistance observed in late adolescence and early adulthood are much more important agents of crime reduction than any known treatment program. Growing up is by far the most potent known cure for crime.

These same patterns are also involved in the reduction of violent crimes such as robbery and assault. But just as there are persistent recidivists among adolescent burglars, so there are violent offenders who display far more intransigence than their age peers. There is no documented tendency for violent juveniles to be any more fixed in their propensity to repeat their offenses than the nonviolent juvenile offenders. Only 17 percent of the former are referred to court for a second violent offense (Snyder 1998). Thus the prospect of spontaneous desistance is a justification for less restrictive responses to violent, as well as to nonviolent, delinquency. Even without any demonstrated treatment effects, a prospect for desistance provides an independent justification for the avoidance of drastic sanctions.

The propensity of a juvenile to accept professional help and juvenile court supervision is regarded as a favorable indication for juvenile court adjudication for two reasons. First, the cooperation of the defendant may reduce the level of crime in the community by making the offender more compliant with the supervision and management of the court. The cooperative juvenile may be a superior actuarial risk, although I know of no rigorous research that has tested this hypothesis. Second, it is human nature for court and probation staff to feel better disposed to those of their clients who cooperate and show respect. In juvenile and criminal courts it is often thought that when defendants are severely punished after multiple failures of probation and supervision, the defendant is punished, in effect, for being in contempt of court.

There has been little systematic research about whether different categories of offenders vary in their acceptance of help and supervision. My guess in that the extreme heterogeneity of violent offenses and offenders generally produces the same variation in the acceptance of help and supervision among them as among nonviolent offenders. If racial minorities are more frequently perceived as non-cooperative, the larger concentration of African-Americans who commit violent offenses might be associated with more recalcitrant defendants.

The Virginia Governor's Commission on Juvenile Justice (1995) isolates one further attribute of suitability for juvenile court jurisdiction—offenses that are typical of the developmental phases of adolescence. Juvenile courts were established, in this view, to cope with law violations that were closely linked in their etiology to the process of being young. In contrast, offenses that are not typical of an adolescent developmental stage seem less suitable for processing by a special court for children and adolescents. This notion of developmentally typical offenses should be distinguished from the simple wish to treat less serious forms of criminality in a juvenile court. The commission restricts its notion of juvenile crime to vandalism and juvenile pranks, thereby invoking a normative rather than a behavioral standard of developmentally typical crime. Yet if there is any independent merit to the juvenile court treatment of developmentally typical juvenile offenses, the standard should encompass serious, as well as trivial, criminal behavior that is distinctively adolescent.

It turns out that violence is a test case of the suitability of juvenile court adjudication for serious but typical adolescent offenses. Very serious fighting, arson, robbery, gross and reckless endangerment, drive-by shootings, drag racing, and other species of outrageously dangerous driving are all typically adolescent behaviors that peak in the middle and late teen years and have high rates of age-related desistance. The behaviors are no less frightening because of their concentration in a single developmental phase, but typicality might still function as an argument for their retention in the juvenile justice system.

The only two characteristics that create tension between serious acts of adolescent violence and the suitability of traditional standards of juvenile justice are the severity of the offense and the dangerousness of the offender. The majority of all juvenile assaults and robberies are not very dangerous acts, but the minority of attacks that are quite serious also constitute the great majority of all juvenile crime that generates the highest social costs. Similarly, most of the youths arrested for violent offenses are not particularly dangerous, but the great majority of all juvenile offenders who are highly dangerous have been arrested for violent crimes while young.

To put the issue in the kind of round numbers that should warn readers about guesswork in progress, between 90 percent and 95 percent of all juveniles arrested for offenses of violence do not substantially diverge from the types of youths and crimes that can be processed and sanctioned by the modern American juvenile court. But about 5 percent to 10 percent of those juveniles arrested for offenses of violence do put special pressure on the principles and processes of juvenile court, usually because of the seriousness of the injuries inflicted by the crime.

A Dubious Double Duty

For the most part, the assaults and robberies that constitute the bulk of youth violence in the United States in the 1990s involve the types of offenses and the types of offenders that the juvenile courts have been processing for at least a generation. The pedigree of assault as a juvenile court behavior is as old as the court itself. If most of this behavior has not changed, why is there a crisis of mission in the juvenile court that has focused on violence? The simple answer is that the violent acts that provoked the rethinking of juvenile justice are the extremely dangerous minority of attacks that threaten or take the lives of their victims. It is the juvenile drive-by shooter who has become the paradigm case, inspiring both easier transfer of serious offenders to criminal courts and a punitive reframing of the principles of juvenile court.

It is both natural and appropriate that extreme cases command a disproportionate share of public and legislative attention. But the double duty performed by the specter of the juvenile killer is curious in one respect. Since virtually all states have liberalized the standards for transfer to the criminal courts to accommodate homicide cases, the juvenile killer should be removed from consideration when taking account of the orientation and sanctions of the juvenile justice system. That is, Willie Horton, Jr., is not a juvenile justice problem because he will not appear in the juvenile court. Thus public fears about these extreme cases should be irrelevant in any jurisdiction that allows transfer.

The drive-by shooter, however, is currently functioning as a symbol of all juvenile violence, and not infrequently as a symbol of all juvenile crime. The result is that we currently make removal of serious offenders from the juvenile court a high priority and then forget that we provided for such removal when we restructure the procedures and standards of the juvenile court. The worst cases of juvenile violence are now performing a dubious double duty in the debate about violence.

The Penalty Gap and Blended Jurisdiction

When observers conclude that a particular offense is too serious to be disposed of by a juvenile court under its delinquency jurisdiction, the usual meaning of the phrase "too serious" is that the minimum amount of punishment that should be imposed exceeds the maximum amount of incarceration available in juvenile court (Zimring 1991). For those who would deny that the juvenile courts of the United States ever punish offenders the objection would be that the criminal act requires punishment but the juvenile courts can only administer treatment. More worldly observers would admit that the juvenile court administers punishment, but they would emphasize the relatively low upper limits of its punishment power. The juvenile court cannot adjudicate all acts of juvenile violence because there is a penalty gap that would frustrate justice in the most serious cases. One way to close the penalty gap in serious cases is to substantially expand the maximum duration of secure confinement that it can order. If two years in a training school is an insufficient punishment for unpremeditated murder by a 15-year-old, why not increase the maximum custodial sentence to ten years or to fifteen years?

There are, however, both procedural and substantive problems in inreasing punishments without making many other changes in the nature of the juvenile court. The lessened procedural rights of the accused invite concern that basing heavy punishment on fact-finding may be unfair and unjustifiable. To deny a juvenile accused of murder the right to be tried before a jury seems more than problematic when fifteen or twenty years of confinement can be the consequence of a finding of juvenile delinquency in the case. Moreover, long durations of penal confinement, the ten- or twenty-year sentence for the juvenile killer, may be inconsistent with the premises and philosophy of juvenile court. If its processes depend on giving a high priority to the needs and interests of the accused delinquent, massive doses of punishment are inconsistent with its central vision. Twenty-year sentences may be socially unavoidable but could still be inappropriate for a court that must put great weight on the interests of juveniles.

No jurisdiction has substantially expanded the punishment powers of the juvenile court without making other changes in the fact-
finding processes and procedural rights of juveniles charged with the
commission of very serious crimes. In recent years, however, some
states have created special categories of legal procedure in their juvenile courts with substantially expanded maximum punishments.
Beginning with Washington State in 1977 (Schneider and Schram
1983), a handful of states now provide special juvenile court hearings with procedural entitlements for the defendants analogous to
those available in criminal courts and maximum periods of secure
confinement that can extend deep into a defendant's adulthood (see
Feld 1993).

The handful of blended jurisdiction schemes have two characteristics in common—longer maximum custodial sentences and more
extensive procedural rights for the accused—but they differ in other
important respects. The very long sentences handed down in Texas
are conditional rather than determined at the time of the original sentencing, and the prison terms that can exceed thirty years go into effect only after a second judicial hearing that takes place when the offender is too old for the juvenile justice system. The evident theory
here is that the behavior of the offender in the juvenile correctional
system should be an important consideration in whether the adult
sentence is executed. In Massachusetts, in contrast, an extended sentence is given at the original trial and need not be contingent on later
judicial proceedings.

Blended jurisdiction statutes may also differ in the residual availability of transfer to criminal court. In Massachusetts, the extended
punishment powers of juvenile court are the only mechanism available for the additional punishment of aggravated forms of juvenile
crime except for first and second degree murder. In Texas and Minnesota, however, the blended jurisdiction powers operate in tandem
with broader provisions for the transfer of older juvenile defendants
to criminal courts. Thus, hybrid juvenile court procedures and punishments are a substitute for transfer to criminal court in nonhomicide cases in Massachusetts but a supplement to the transfer provisions in Texas and Minnesota.

The different types of blended jurisdiction place substantial limits
on the degree to which general judgments about them have validity.
In some systems, the extended sentence is only a threat; in others, it
has a legal effect not far from the sentences of criminal courts after
trial. In some jurisdictions the practice was created as an exclusive

avenue for enhanced punishment, at least for some types of offenders; in others, the new procedures simply add another layer of penalty to an apparatus that also retains the broad power to transfer to criminal court.

Two questions should be asked about to blended jurisdiction schemes as a response to aggravated forms of juvenile violence. First, do they succeed in closing the penalty gap when ordinary juvenile court sanctions are the only response available for egregiously serious acts of youth violence? Second, do hybrid punishment extensions in juvenile court generate substantial new problems? Most existing systems of blended jurisdiction are problematic on both counts. They do not provide the kind and amount of secure confinement to allow them to function as a credible plenary alternative to criminal court jurisdiction, and they create problems in theory and practice for the cases they are intended to reach and for the overall mission of the juvenile courts that adopt them.

No state has adopted an expanded set of punishment powers in juvenile court as a binding alternative to transferring juveniles to criminal court. All the systems that use blended jurisdiction hedge their bets by also providing for criminal court transfer in defined classes of extremely serious juvenile violence.

The legislative distrust of blended jurisdiction may be related to the conditional nature of extended punishment in hybrid systems other than Massachusetts. Only the Massachusetts system gives its court the power to issue a durational sentence with the same binding force as that provided by a criminal court. In Texas and Minnesota, the adult sentence imposed at the time of adjudication is a threat, not a promise, a threat that may be avoided by good behavior in the juvenile correctional system.

A legislature might distrust the threats represented by conditional sentences for two reasons. First, it might view the long but conditional sentence as a license for judicial bluffing—a system deliberately designed to pronounce long sentences but avoid their effect. In an age where "truth in sentencing" is a popular sound bite, conditional sentencing may look like its opposite. This may be acceptable to a legislature when conditional sentences only add to the punishments currently available, but there may be unwillingness to abolish other punitive options as an even trade for the punishment that conditional sentences might provide.

Second, the theory gap is a philosophical misfit between the retributive feelings that lead to a punishment gap and the programmatic or rehabilitative rationale that is the only plausible justification for making long custodial sentences conditional. If a 15-year-old student shoots his eighth-grade mathematics teacher, why give him a sentence of two and one-half years that might be extended thirty-seven more years at a later judicial hearing? If the reasons for requiring longer sentences have to do with the gravity of the crime, there might seem to be no additional advantage in waiting to make a final punishment determination.

Some Disadvantages

The creation of separate procedures and penalties to accommodate cases of serious violence carries a variety of costs. Conflict between the principles that animate decisions in blended cases and the general principles of the delinquency jurisdiction produces a cognitive dissonance for judges, lawyers, and probation officers. Two different kinds of courts for young offenders that function under the same roof and use the same personnel create a confusion of purpose. Once principles of lessened priority for the interests of the individual juvenile and extended punishment power establish a beachhead in the juvenile court, there is no easily defensible border between conventional delinquency approaches and the premises of the blended jurisdiction. If armed robbers should be subject to the extended penalties and enhanced procedures, why not all robbers? If robbers are appropriate for a blended jurisdiction, why not residential burglars? Once we have institutionalized a set of principles in juvenile court that compete with the usual approach, the barrier between aggravated and standard delinquency can be lowered by increments on a never-ending basis. The principles that underlie blended jurisdiction are by no means self-limiting, and they could cover a very wide spectrum of crime.

Therefore, one set of negative consequences that can flow from blended jurisdiction is a continuing tension and discomfort associated with trying to administer two inconsistent sanctioning systems side by side. A second set of negative consequences will arise if the new approach displaces the old, so that a much larger category of offenses and offenders is subject to blended jurisdiction.

What benefits can offset these dangers and costs? The case for blended jurisdiction is almost always framed in pragmatic rather than principled terms. From the standpoint of the institutional interests of juvenile court, changing the terms of its jurisdiction might be preferable to losing jurisdiction over important categories of cases. From the standpoint of juveniles accused of very serious offenses, the extended punishments of blended jurisdiction might be the lesser of two evils. A long sentence from a juvenile court is considered preferable to a long sentence imposed by a criminal court, particularly if most of the blended sentence is conditional. The pragmatic argument is that the justice system is less compromised by extended sentences in juvenile court than by higher frequencies of waiver to criminal court. The juvenile defendants may also be better off if the punitive bite of the blended jurisdiction sentence is less than the sanction that would have been imposed if blended jurisdiction were not available.

This rationale rests on empirical assertions that have never been rigorously evaluated. Does the availability of blended jurisdiction rescue a large number of juvenile offenders from transfer into the criminal courts? How many? How many of the new blended jurisdiction defendants would not have been transferred to criminal court if only standard delinquency and criminal court options existed? The available evidence on these matters is charitably viewed as inconclusive. In Texas, the volume of transfers to criminal court increased fourfold in the first decade of blended jurisdiction, from about 125 cases per year in 1985 and 1986 to an average of 573 cases per year in 1994, 1995, and 1996 (Texas Department of Juvenile Probation 1984–1986, 1994–1996). There is no way of assessing the volume of transfers that might have occurred if no blended jurisdiction options were available, but the high numbers are not good news for the diversionary power of blended jurisdiction. In Minnesota, there was no Texas-style growth in transfers, but it is difficult to tell whether this trend is evidence that blended jurisdiction is working well or that it was not needed.

Despite the empirical uncertainties, three conclusions are supported by experience to date. First, even those systems that are successful in rescuing some serious offenders from worse fates can achieve that result only by putting other accused delinquents at greater risk. Even if some juveniles accused of homicide or rape benefit from blended jurisdiction, instead of criminal court, a number of other juveniles accused of robbery and gun assault will be upgraded from ordinary delinquency proceedings to the larger risks of blended jurisdiction. Introducing the intermediate option in juvenile court is certain to elevate the consequences faced by some accused juveniles. The group at hazard might be relatively small in systems that vigorously restrict capacity in blended jurisdiction. If the assumptions and principles of blended jurisdiction become the dominant orientation of juvenile court in delinquency cases, however, the number of accused delinquents who are put at extra risk by blended jurisdiction would be extremely large. Thus, even if some juveniles benefit from blended jurisdiction, others, those with somewhat less serious charges, will be put at increased hazard as a consequence.

Second, the only reason to graft this system onto juvenile court is the assumption that a larger measure of youth protection can be achieved in the juvenile courts than by legislative and institutional adjustments in the criminal courts. Richard Redding (1997) argues that extending punishment powers in juvenile courts is good because it preserves the rehabilitative treatment that can be offered there. Yet there is no logical reason that such features as separate institutions for youths, special sentences for young offenders, and conditional terms of penal confinement have to be restricted to juvenile courts. Many youth-specific sentencing and correctional regimes have been incorporated by criminal courts. The argument for blended jurisdiction rests on a political rather than a penological hypothesis. The notion is that more juvenile-friendly substantive outcomes may be achieved in legislation if the changes advocated are directed at juvenile rather than criminal courts.

The largest risk concerns the juvenile court itself. If the principles of blended jurisdiction are inconsistent with the operational philosophy of the juvenile court, bringing blended jurisdiction into the court introduces a competing set of principles for all cases. To the extent that ideologies depend on internal consistency, the introduction of competitive principles into juvenile court may be its undoing. However, the only way blended jurisdictional schemes can successfully ward off mass transfers to criminal courts is to promise results that are more punitive than the ordinary outcomes of juvenile justice. The dilemma is that such systems will be politically ineffective (if the principles of the new system are not inconsistent with juvenile justice) or dangerous (if their principles are inconsistent with juvenile justice in general). It is not unthinkable that some versions of blended jurisdiction might be both ineffective and dangerous.

The Tail That Wags the Dog

Trends in the rate and character of youth violence in the United States provide no reason for a shift in the operating philosophy of the juvenile court in delinquency cases. The violent cases the court saw in 1997 are, for the most part, the same mix that it processed in 1977. There have been increases in the number of homicide arrests—at the top of the seriousness scale—and larger increases in the assault and aggravated assault arrests at the bottom. With such a heterogeneous mix of offenses, talk of an "average" violent offense is not very helpful, although the data reviewed in chapter 3 indicate that the average juvenile arrest for violent crime in the mid-1990s is probably less serious than fifteen or twenty years earlier. The reason is that marginal cases are being classified as aggravated, and less serious assaults are now more likely to result in arrest.

If the typical violent juvenile is not a good reason to reorient the juvenile court, what about the worst cases of youth violence? Drive-by killers are obviously a poor model for juvenile court reform. They will not be tried in a juvenile court and are not representative of delinquents in general or of violent delinquents in particular. The worst cases of youth violence have always been removed from juvenile to criminal courts, and recent legislative activity has increased the use of transfer. It is thus ludicrous to design a set of juvenile court processes to handle offenders who will in fact be tried elsewhere. The 16-year-old juvenile killer is currently being used as an absentee exemplar for reforming a set of institutions that will never try this defendent. Whatever may be the correct way to rethink the mission of the juvenile court, basing sanctions and procedures on nonexistent juvenile court cases must be wrong.

But what about the next most serious cases—the 15-year-old who wounds with a gun but does not kill? The marginal accomplice to a killing? The repeat armed robber? The two trends in recent years for such cases are to increase the volume and rate of waiver or to create special subdivisions of the juvenile court empowered to deliver much longer custodial sentences. If the interests of the accused can be protected as effectively in criminal court, transfer would be the obvious preference. Avoiding the dissonance of a two-track delinquency jurisdiction and protecting those accused of less serious robberies and burglaries from the magnetic force of an aggravated delinquency category are reasons why blended jurisdiction is hazardous to the mission of the juvenile court and the interests of other juvenile offenders. It is only when we are powerless to moderate the punitive bite of the criminal courts after transfer occurs that the conflict between the interests of juvenile robbers and those of juvenile burglars becomes intractable.

The only effective way to protect the integrity of the juvenile court in such circumstances is to maintain a capacity in criminal court to moderate the penal policies that apply to young offenders. The false dichotomy of protecting youths in juvenile court while ignoring immaturity in criminal court is more than a threat to the coherence of the system as a whole. It also puts distortive pressure on juvenile court. Bending the limits of juvenile justice to accommodate especially serious cases creates a conflict of purpose in the court, as well as substantial danger of punitive contagion. For this reason, rationality in juvenile court may ultimately depend on the other institutions of criminal justice having coherent policies for young offenders. If the juvenile courts function as isolated islands of policy toward young offenders, they are in constant danger.

The analysis in this chapter is not meant to be a comprehensive apology for the operation of juvenile courts in the mid-1990s. There may be a variety of good reasons to rethink all legal policies for adolescent offenders. One might argue that modern juvenile justice may have been a bad idea all along. But this chapter concerns a more limited question: Have recent trends in youth violence undermined the conceptual or empirical foundations for delinquency jurisdiction in juvenile court? The answer is no.

Youth Violence
and Youth Policy

This book is about a subject of only modest importance.
Just as violence is a small part of the process of growing
up, government policy toward youth violence is not a major element
in the complex of government policies that influence the development and welfare of young persons in the United States. Although a
substantial minority of American boys are involved in fights and assaults, for the most part these are not important developmental mile-
stones and the transition away from violence is a normal part of social maturation. The legal rules that have major impact on adolescent
development in the United States concern education, job training,
medical care, employment, and driving privileges. Policy toward
youth violence should be only a small piece of a large puzzle. It
should be consistent with the general principles that inform youth
policy in its many other contexts, but it should not govern youth
development.

What sets off current conditions in the United States as peculiar is
that the sentiments expressed in the previous paragraph are now
controversial. Youth violence is believed to be a proper basis for general policies toward adolescents. Critics on the right use concern
about serious crime to render undesirable a future generation of adolescents who are presently small children. Critics on the left suggest
that social policies intended to nurture and support youth development should be packaged as crime prevention. There is apparent
agreement in these two positions that questions relating to adolescent violence should play a major role in government policy toward
the young.

That view is wrong. This concluding essay is an attempt to restore
perspective to the role of youth violence concerns in determining
legal policies toward adolescents. The first section speculates about
the factors that have produced the rise in concern to embarrassing
prominence. The second section shows how a peculiarity in the psy-

chology of intergenerational comparison has contributed to the pessimism we feel about the outlook for teenagers ten and fifteen years in the future. The third section offers a critique of crime prevention motives as a selling point for government services to the young. The fourth section views the crime scare of the 1990s as a failure of perspective.

Hope is the necessary fuel for effective youth welfare programs; fear is a corrupting and ultimately destructive influence on programs intended to promote youth welfare. The less prominent the role of crime prevention in the construction of youth policy, the better the youth policy.

The Year 1998 as a Rhetorical Moment

Recent congressional speeches about teenage violence in the year 2010 were problematic in a number of respects. Some of the problems have already been discussed in earlier chapters: The rate of serious violence to be expected from a population now under the age of 5 is unknowable because rates of violence fluctuate in cycles that are not susceptible to long-range prediction. Also, many of the factors that will influence the youth violence rate ten and fifteen years from now have not yet taken shape. The proximate causes of rates of homicide and deadly assault among 17-year-olds in 2010 are events that will occur in 2008 and 2009. Good predictions of rates of serious violence require the services not merely of a demographer but of a clairvoyant as well. Furthermore, the growth of the youth population in the first decade of the next century is far short of baby-boom adolescents. The 16 percent expansion of middle teenagers that will occur over fifteen years will produce a number of teens in 2010 no greater than the absolute number in the United States in 1975, and the proportion of the population in the age group 13–17 will remain much smaller than during the 1960s and 1970s.

Beyond these tactical concerns, which are discussed in earlier chapters, two more fundamental problems merit close attention. First, adolescent violence has shifted to a position of central importance in discussing the prospects for an emerging generation of youths and the government policies that should be devised to meet changing needs. The *only* aspect of the youth population in 2010 that has been examined in Congress over the years since 1996 has been juvenile arrest and crime trends. Thus criminality has become the primary characteristic of interest to the federal legislature in planning for policy toward young persons in the next fifteen years.

This crime-centered approach comes not from police or juvenile court agencies, with a professional specialization that would lead us to expect a narrow emphasis on crime, but from legislative representatives with broad responsibilities. Representative McCollum's (1996) warnings of juvenile predations were delivered at a hearing of the House Subcommittee on Early Childhood, Youth, and Families. Youth violence was not merely the most important element in juvenile justice policy in 1997, but it was also the most important topic in congressional consideration of youth policy in general. This is big news and bad news for the United States. The preoccupation with children then 2 and 3 years old did not involve government services such as education and training but rather the terrible crimes that the teens of fifteen years hence might commit. Only a Senate initiative to finance children's health care with cigarette taxes received the same level of attention as serious youth crime in 2010.

A second major difficulty is linked to the fact that violent crime has a central role in thinking about the prospects for future generations of adolescents. A modest expansion in the size of the youth population is regarded as unqualified bad news. It is never alleged that more than a small proportion of this population will be involved in serious criminality, but this is the only subject to be considered in congressional debate. From this perspective, an entire generation of future adolescents is considered to be bad news, so that the larger the size of the cohort, the bigger the social and government problems that will result.

Cause or Effect?

How does it happen that a child-centered and optimistic culture embraces such a narrow and negative view of a future generation in prosperous times? One theory is that this view is driven by a fear of violent youth crime that has spread to cities and suburbs in the 1990s. If fear of crime is on the increase, however, it is flourishing in spite of a downward trend in violent attacks. It is by no means impossible for anxieties about violent crime to move in the opposite direction from crime rates, but such an inverse pattern must itself involve some immediate inducement to fear other than increasing rates of violence. Could it be media attention? Or, indeed, could this anxiety be driven by fear-arousing rhetoric about future juvenile predators from politicians and opinion leaders?

This suggests a contrasting scenario, one in which the negative predictions about future youth cohorts are as much the cause of anxiety as they are the effect of current fears and experience (Beckett 1997). Indeed, one way to justify a negative view of an emerging generation is to focus on a negative attribute such as crime. Even if only 6 percent or 3 percent of a population is highly criminal, its overall prospects will not look good if crime is the only characteristic that is discussed. To keep the focus on crime and crime alone, then is to guarantee a negative impression of future prospects

But why select a negative characteristic as a single-issue crystal ball? One motive for concentrating on antisocial behavior is to justify hostile attitudes or actions. Justice Oliver Wendell Holmes famously used this device to justify involuntary sterilization procedures in Virginia public hospitals. About the births this policy was to prevent, Holmes argued: "It is better for all the world, if instead of waiting to execute degenerate offspring for crime, or to let them starve for their imbecility, society can prevent those who are manifestly unfit from continuing their kind" (*Buck v. Bell*, 274 U.S. 201, 1927). The rhetoric of Holmes reminds us that a focus on the future threat of crime may be not only a result of anxiety but also an attempt to create fear of the young. Thus worry about crime and violence is both a cause and an effect of a crime-centered view of tomorrow's youths.

It is not easy to determine how much of the current concern is chiefly a rhetorical justification for preemptive hostility in government policy and how much is crime-driven anxiety without any preset policy agenda. To some extent the language selected to describe the future threat may reveal the nature of the speaker's feelings. To speak of the never born as "imbeciles" bound for execution is consistent with preemptive hostility, and the same may hold for current labels like "juvenile super predator" and "feral pre-social being." But even martial language cannot completely separate ad hominem agendas from merely anxious ones because many citizens regard future generations of American youths with genuinely mixed feelings, which overlap neat boundaries. The sentiments many of us express about young people are rendered oblique by more than insincerity. There is real confusion and ambivalence in the attitudes of the general public and of many elected officials.

One further confounding factor is the attitude toward young

blacks and Hispanics. Fear of violent young offenders is almost always a fear of other people's children and has been throughout the
twentieth-century history of the United States. By the early 1980s,
the racial and ethnic differences between the generations in urban
areas were compounding intergenerational tensions. In the 1980 census, more than 60 percent of those under 18 in New York City had
dark skins or spoke Spanish, whereas more than 60 percent of those
over 18 did not (Zimring 1982:Chap. 12). In the 1990 census, black
and Hispanic youths were the majority of all those under 18 in four
of the five largest cities but a majority of the adult population in none
of them. White non-Hispanics are only 30.6 percent of the youth
population in these cities but 46 percent of the adult population
(U.S. Department of Commerce 1990). Similar racial and ethnic differences can be found in most major cities in the 1990s, and the
image of the violent juvenile offender, now and in the future, is that
of a dark-skinned stranger.

There are manifold effects of the racial and ethnic differences between the citizens now being invited to worry about future youth
violence and the people they are being invited to worry about. When
the citizens' sense of the "otherness" of black and Hispanic youths is
strong, they may not identify with these potential criminals in the
same way they are likely to identify with children and youths in
their own families and affinity groups. Not only is there less positive
identification, but also there are fewer barriers to the negative stereotypes being applied. It is hard to imagine the child down the block as
tomorrow's superpredator. But wherever racial dividing lines are
important—and that condition holds in every American city—the
racial and ethnic division between the young and the adult encour-
ages negative stereotypes and cartoon superficiality in the motives
and character we project onto youths.

A Self-fulfilling Prophecy?

Once public attention has been directed toward the specter of youth
violence, media exposure can contribute to increased fear even when
rates of violence are not increasing. Most citizens get their crime
news second- and third-hand in the United States, and impressions
formed in this way may depend as much on the amount of coverage
in the media as on violence in one's neighborhood or hometown. The
news media are market-driven; what events receive attention depends in large measure on what interests and concerns the citizen.

To the extent that news producers believe citizens are concerned about youth violence, extensive coverage of violent acts can be expected to increase; moreover, the youthfulness of the assailants will become a focus of media attention if very young offenders are of increased concern to the citizens who participate in surveys and focus groups. Thus citizens' fears produce more coverage of youth violence and more emphasis on violent acts when the offenders are quite young. This increased coverage and emphasis will produce more concern among citizens, which in turn will increase the salience of violent youths in the news.

The selection biases of news producers may be innocent—indeed the essence of democratic accountability—but the result is a vicious circle in which crime rates can stand still while public fears and media attention create self-sustaining processes of escalating concern and coverage. But won't news stories about crime trends break this tendency? The problem here may be that crime statistics are not as newsworthy as crimes, and the supply of murders, rapes, robberies, and shootings is endless in most major media markets. Only if statistical information functions as a corrective, a sort of firebreak on the worries generated by event coverage, can the reciprocal increases in public concern and media attention be moderated.

There are two plausible relationships between the objective measurement of a particular phenomenon, such as youth violence, and the level of public concern about it at a particular time. The first pattern is nearly total independence. An increasing rate of youth homicides may play an important role in starting a cycle of public concern and media coverage, but after that launch public concern might fluctuate in response to noncrime factors. In this model, crime trends act like kindling wood, but the size and duration of the fire of public alarm are determined by the supply of other types of fuel, manifestations of public concern like media coverage and political attention.

Public worry about youth crime, however, is not in a process of perpetual increase. What stops the cycle if not declining crime rates? It may be that the attention span of the public on a particular topic is finite, so that media messages have diminishing marginal impact after protracted exposure. Or the public may become susceptible to distraction by other pressing concerns: The percentage of Americans who thought that drugs were the most important domestic problem fell rapidly as an economic recession took center stage in the early 1990s (Zimring and Hawkins 1992).

The second pattern is a casual relationship between crime trends and public worry, complicated by a time lag. Rates of youth violence increase for a time before gaining media and public attention. Then the reciprocal reinforcements of media coverage and public concern may continue to increase public worries even after the level of youth violence has passed its peak. But sooner or later, both media coverage and public fear respond to the objectively measured realities of the threat of violence. It may take years for perceptions to catch up with trends, but the actual trends in crime are eventual influences on levels of public concern. Facts have a major influence on public concerns—if you wait long enough.

The years since 1995 provide an opportunity to see whether delayed reaction or lack of a crime trend influence explains the persistence of increasing concern about youth violence during a period of sustained good news about violence of all kinds. Between 1992 and 1996, the homicide rate in the United States declined by almost 25 percent to a level not experienced since 1969. As discussed in chapter 3, youth homicide, which can be traced only through arrests, peaked in 1993 but then fell faster in the next three years than the general homicide rate had fallen during its five-year decline. The largest annual decline was in 1995, right in the middle of the moral panic about youth violence. By the end of 1996, almost two-thirds of the total increase in juvenile homicide rates over their 1980 level had been erased by the three year decline. What remains to be measured are trends in television coverage of acts of youth violence and trends in levels of public concern. This is a natural experiment that can provide insight into the dynamics of public anxiety on specific issues.

From Perception to Reality

None of the preceding analysis directly addresses the argument that the youth cohorts that will enter adolescence over the next ten to fifteen years are at particular risk for high rates of life-threatening violence. Most of the preceding analysis operates independently of the volume of violence we can expect from future teens. It would be ludicrous to focus mainly on an emerging generation's juvenile homicide rate even if annual homicide arrests for 14- to 17-year-olds were to climb from the rate of 1 in 9,000 in 1996 to 1 in 6,000 in 1993. Emphasis on a single issue disserves the public interest under any circumstances of expected youth violence.

But what do we know about the general developmental prospects of this year's kindergartners? How does this information affect our capacity to predict juvenile violence ten and fifteen years in the future? And what should we do to reduce the hazards for children who will be making the transition to adolescence in the coming decade? The next section makes some general observations about the prospects of very young children in the United States in 1997. The section that follows argues that even the best-intentioned efforts to promote child welfare in the guise of categorical crime prevention programs would be a policy mistake.

A Generation at Risk?

Pessimistic assessments of the prospects of young persons are by no means a novelty of recent vintage or an American invention. Fear that the nation's youths are headed for serious trouble is a perennial theme of intergenerational relationships and is particularly pronounced in times of rapid social change. The current wave of worry about youth violence in the future shares two elements with the standard adult anxieties that one encounters in the widest diversity of social and political circumstances—an emphasis on moral disability and a negative selection bias in the characteristics emphasized when current youths are compared with their predecessors.

Where the current concerns differ from the general run of generational worries is in focusing specifically on crime and in advocating preemptive preparation of countermeasures. It turns out, however, that the evidence in support of the current intergenerational bad dream is not closely connected to crime rates or to any specific birth cohort among the parade of future adolescent generations in the United States. The current concern about future trends is more typical of standard complaints about the future than its authors would acknowledge.

It is beyond dispute that trouble lies in the path of the most disadvantaged quarter of the children that will become adolescents in the first decade of the twenty-first century in the United States. Moreover, disproportionate involvement in juvenile arrests is usually found among disadvantaged youths, along with higher than average rates of educational difficulty, leaving school, health problems, and unemployment. What beyond these general tendencies might provide evidence that a cohort of 4-year-olds will create a wave of violence when they are 16?

In many of the analyses, "the coming storm of juvenile violence" was solely a statistical extrapolation of 1993 rates of violence into the expanding volume of young persons projected by 2010 (see Snyder and Sickmund 1995; Fox 1996; and chapter 4). Why a future youth population might be expected to offend at the 1993 rate, or at any other rate, is not indicated. Because this year's 2-year-olds have not demonstrated propensities for involvement in violent crime, long-range predictions of high crime rates should be based on the presence of characteristics that are regarded as reliable antecedents to violence later in life or on environmental conditions that are associated with predictable rates of violent crime.

Some of the "coming storm" commentaries have included arguments about high-risk antecedent conditions to violence to be found in large groups of young children in the United States. One risk factor widely cited is the large number of single-parent or fatherless children. Bennett et al. (1996), who coined the phrase "the coming storm of juvenile violence," tie the structural conditions like single-parent families to a criminally antecedent condition they call "moral poverty":

> By "moral poverty" we mean the poverty of being without loving, capable, responsible adults who teach the young right from wrong. [Living in] the poverty of being without parents, guardians, relatives, friends, teachers, coaches, clergy who habituate . . . children. It is the poverty of growing up in the virtual absence of people who teach these lessons by their own everyday example, and who insist that you follow suit and behave accordingly. (pp. 13–14)

The antecedent conditions that are links to "moral poverty" in this type of analysis seem quite similar to structural characteristics that social scientists on the left also identify as a particular worry in recent decades: high rates of out-of-wedlock childbirth and one-parent (usually fatherless) families and family disorganization and instability. The rate of single-parent households has been rising quickly in the United States, as it has also in other Western nations since the 1960s.

Family disorganization is an important risk factor for crime and delinquency, as is single-parent status. Does that mean that the general crime rate should increase because the proportion of single-parent families has increased? Should variations in the risk of delinquency predict variations in the rate of life-threatening violence? The answer to both these questions is "not necessarily."

First, the fact that a characteristic is a risk factor for delinquent acts does not mean that variations in the rate of the characteristic will be reflected in a higher general rate of crime. Males with a single parent might be more likely than those with two parents to be arrested for car theft, but that does not mean that an increase in the single-parent percentage will necessarily increase the general rate of car theft (see Zimring and Hawkins 1997: App. 1). Whether and to what extent increases in risk factors for individuals also increase the crime rates of whole populations is still an open question. Large decreases in youth crime have occurred twice since 1980, in 1980–1984 and 1993–1996, without any shift in family structure to explain them.

Second, making the jump from juvenile delinquency to high rates of life-threatening violence is clearly not warranted by current facts. Illegitimate births, single-parent families, and other measures of family disorganization greatly increased in Britain in the 1970s and 1980s, but the homicide rate dropped substantially afterward (compare United Kingdom Office of National Statistics 1997:Table 2.3 with Zimring and Hawkins 1997:240). This does not, of course, mean that single-parent families and lack of supportive family organization are anything other than risk factors for negative outcomes in Britain. However, the immediate social context in which children enter adolescence will determine what sorts of negative outcomes most often emerge. There is no inevitable connection between the level of either family structure or measurable moral learning and the rate of later violence.

Cohort Versus Environmental Influence on Violence

The general tendency is for rates of serious violence of all high-risk age groups to rise and fall together rather than for different age groups to experience different trends at the same time. The homicide rate among teens aged 14 to 17 was supposed to be an exception to this rule in the late 1980s and early 1990s because the homicide rates of many older groups were going down. Even in this time period, however, the trends for 14- to 17-year-olds were almost exactly the same as the trends for those 18 to 24 (Cook and Laub 1998). When many different age groups have simultaneous upward and downward movements in homicide rates, this is strong evidence that changing conditions in the environments, which different age groups share, are responsible rather than the risk characteristics of one particular group. It has been widely thought that only teenage violence rates were increasing in the late 1980s (Bennett et al. 1996:13), which could have been evidence that the characteristics of one narrow age group were responsible. But the broader age span of even the most recent trends argues against the cohort effect.

So, too, does the sharp drop in homicide among youths noted from 1994 through 1996. Population features like family structure and the concrete determinants of moral poverty are not subject to wide cyclical fluctuations over short periods of time. When the youth homicide arrest rate drops by one-third in three years, the rapid up-and-down swings suggest that environmental conditions, which change quickly, are the immediate cause. If single parenting caused the homicide rate in 1980 to double by 1993, what demographic change would we expect to have caused two-thirds of the rate increase to melt away after 1993? If moral poverty is an increasing phenomenon in the United States and a proximate cause for increasing youth homicide, is the sharp homicide decline strong evidence that the forces of moral poverty are in sudden retreat?

Some might argue that long-term negative trends may influence the cyclical fluctuations in homicide rates by increasing the average level of homicide that is also affected by up-and-down cycles over time. This may be true. If most of the increases and decreases are the result of cyclical fluctuation, however, this modified claim can take credit only for whatever secular increases remain when the cyclical fluctuations are discounted. There is no strong evidence of any upward youth trend for two of the four violent crimes—rape and robbery, although some upward underlying trend in homicide was present in the seventeen years before 1997. Data from the next three or four years may tell us more about homicide trends. Of course, why general conditions such as single-parent families or inadequate moral tuition would increase the rates of only two of four crimes of violence is another question that the proponents of such relationships must address.

At present, the evidence is weak for a clear causal link between long-term trends in family structure or moral education and short-term movements in rates of juvenile violence. This is by no means a certificate of assurance for the future generations of American youths. Inadequate moral training, family disorganization, lack of supervision, and many other current trends are not good news for an emerging generation. But transforming the legitimate general concerns about such developmental deficits into a crime and violence scare is unwarranted and misleading.

Indeed, the current congressional emphasis on a coming storm of juvenile violence underestimates the variety of risks that inadequate support for youths can produce. The precise areas where youth problems are likely to be most prevalent will depend on the particular social environment of a cohort's adolescent years. It is unlikely that an explosive expansion in youth crime and violence would occur in the absence of other major problems. Health problems, education shortfalls, and poor economic prospects would all result from youth deficits of the magnitude to launch a wave of juvenile violence. Concerns about the prospects of today's 2-year-olds would seem more authentic if they involved the multiple social results of deficiencies in the nurturance of young children in the United States. To worry only about the criminal aspects of fatherless families smacks of crocodile tears.

The Pessimistic Bias

Concern for the particularly difficult prospects of the next generation may be premature in one important respect. There is a pronounced tendency for comparisons between generational problems to disfavor the new cohort because the only attributes selected for comparison are current problems. If we are worried about single-parent families and homicide rates, we will compare current and past generations only on these two dimensions; but because we select only those conditions that are current concerns, we virtually guarantee that this year's youths appear to be in difficult straits. It will not reassure a parent currently worried about drive-by shootings that today's generation of American children are far less likely to die in car crashes than those a generation ago. In fact, the death rate for children aged 5 to 14 has dropped by half in the United States over the last generation, and even teenagers are somewhat more likely to survive to adulthood in the 1990s than in the 1960s (Zimring 1997).

High school graduation rates, the prevalence of college training, and other measures of broad educational participation have improved over time. African-American youths still have lower educational attainments and higher death rates than whites, yet their experience has moved in the same positive direction as the general rate and their educational progress in high school and college has been one of the great success stories of the past generation (Patterson 1997). It was not too long ago—the early 1960s—when African-American youths grew up in a nation where official racism was government policy. Even more recently, the combination of compulsory military service and the Vietnam War threatened America's young men with the nonremote prospect of coming home from a foreign nation in a body bag. Not all trends for youths are negative.

When we try to impress our children with the hardships of an older generation's transition to adulthood, we tend to remember only the problems of previous times. When we worry about current and future generations, we focus only on those conditions that most provoke our fears. The selective psychology of intergenerational comparisons can be profoundly misleading. It is possible, however, to gain a perspective on our worries by recognizing the way in which current comparisons have selected only those dimensions that reinforce our fears.

Selling Youth Development as Crime Prevention

Rhetoric about the danger of increased violence has been for the most part a tactic to promote punitive changes in criminal codes and juvenile courts in the United States. The usual counterattack of youth advocates and juvenile justice personnel has been to downplay the accuracy of the predictions or the relevance of arrest rates as a basis for policy. But one recent reaction has seized on fears about future crime to motivate broad welfare programs as instruments of crime prevention.

A major conflict in Congress in the 1990s concerned what types of federal financial support should be emphasized in a comprehensive crime package. From 1991 to 1994, the conservative emphasis was on prison construction, longer and less modifiable criminal sentences, and reduction of legal barriers to swift execution of death sentences. The liberal response emphasized gun control, financial assistance to increase the number of police officers, and aid for prevention programs that were epitomized in the media as "midnight basketball" programs intended to keep potentially troublesome young men out of harm's way. The crime legislation that passed in late 1993 and 1994 was an all-inclusive assortment of strategies from both conservative and liberal agendas—not so much a compromise program as a promiscuous assortment of every pressure group's pet program without any coordination or common strategic approach.

Juvenile crime and juvenile justice were not a high priority in the 1994 act, but the struggle between ideological factions and the

Democrats' attempt to coopt crime fears rather than to downplay them became a preview of the juvenile justice debates in 1996 and 1997. The all-inclusive compromise of the 1994 legislation did not satisfy the Republican legislators, who took control of the Congress in that year's November elections. "Midnight basketball" was a prime target of efforts to amend the crime bill early in 1995.

A second installment of the prevention versus punishment debate took place in California. Early in 1994, the California legislature passed a "Three strikes and you're out" set of mandatory sentences that was vastly more inclusive and expensive than any other modern recidivist sentencing legislation. Peter Greenwood and his associates (1996) at the Rand Corporation prepared estimates of the number of serious crimes prevented per million dollars of public funds spent for this scheme and four different supervision and child services programs. The estimates produced in that report are presented in figure 10.1.

According to the Rand report, the two most effective nonpunishment programs would generate crime savings per million dollars many times those estimated for "three strikes," and at least one of the children's services programs would achieve much less crime prevention per million dollars than the "three strikes" program. The estimates were presented as a criticism of the effectiveness of mandatory sentences as crime control rather than as a specific program of prevention initiatives. The attempt was to create a common basis of comparison, the relative costs per crime avoided, for a broad variety of crime control measures. There was no suggestion in the report that funding for home visits and day care should stand or fall on its crime prevention impact.

The "midnight basketball" controversy and the Rand analysis can be seen as examples of prevention programs in a competion with punishment for financial resources that were to be dedicated to crime control objectives in any event. In each case, the conflict was about how money earmarked for crime control could best be spent. The prevention advocates were not making demands on new resources or claiming that the crime problem demanded a larger response. Also, the programs featured as most cost-effective were targeted at high-risk candidates and during high-risk periods of adolescence.

But why not channel public fear of youth crime to expand the support for programs designed to help young people? When the "coming storm" refrain was enlisted in the cause of punitive responses to juvenile crime, some of the demographic forecasters

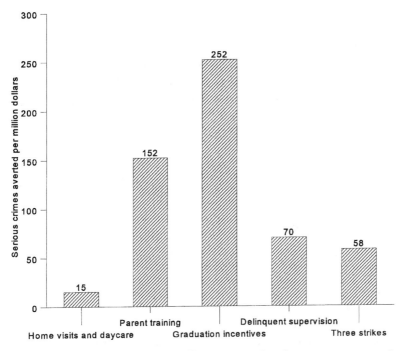

Figure 10.1. Comparison of Cost Effectiveness of Early Interventions with California's Three-Strikes Law, 1996. Source: Greenwood et al. (1996).

sought to disassociate themselves from that rhetoric and make the pessimistic projections into an argument for more welfare. James Allen Fox of Northeastern University, a criminologist who had coined the term "bloodbath" to describe projected rates of adolescent homicide arrests in 2010, emphasized societal neglect as a spin on his statistical projection: *"Given our wholesale disinvestment in youth,* we will likely have more than 5,000 teen killers per year" was his prophecy for the first decade of the twenty-first century (Gest and Pope 1996:29; emphasis added). One inference from this phrasing is that undoing the neglect might yet avoid the catastrophic consequences projected fourteen years into the future. A society with 5,000 teen killers is like a vision in Charles Dickens's *A Christmas Carol,* a frightening view of what will occur if repentance is not quickly achieved. If "disinvestment" is the cause of the teenage bloodbath yet to come, then vigorous investment in youth welfare might be the path to salvation. This tactic might be seen as an adult version of "scared straight," the infamous program in which teen offenders are exposed to the deprivations of prison life in an effort to motivate their reform. What is sauce for the youth is sauce also for the legislator.

The potential for merchandising programs to broadly protect and develop young persons as necessary methods of crime control was the subject of more detailed and more candid advocacy by Bryan Vila (1997). His argument was that the public should be led to support youth welfare by focusing on its crime prevention function:

> Strong support from public and from elected officials is impera-
> tive for the long-term survival of nurturant crime control pro-
> grams. Given the proper marketing strategy, this might be possi-
> ble if child development programs were sold to the public as
> crime control strategies.

I think this would be dangerous salesmanship, however, destructive of the values the author wishes to preserve. The tactic of selling child development programs as crime control is simultaneously ineffective and destructive—ineffective because angry and frightened citizens do not want to wait fifteen years for results and are unwilling to reward threatening children with special benefits; destructive because history teaches us that the one sure way to make such programs fail is to call them crime control. Long-range programs of youth development cannot compete effectively for the resources currently directed into prisons and police. One problem is that fear and anger demand immediate responses, not long-range plans. But there are further problems. When taxpayers are afraid of other people's children, they are much more willing to pay for social control than for youth development.

Reformers once innocently believed that many of the resources that supported detention centers could be redirected toward nonsecure drop-in centers, where the same youths who were once locked up could come and go, finding asylum from street life when they wanted it. It turned out, however, that the willingness to spend money for voluntary support was much lower than the willingness to fund detention (Zimring 1982:69–75) because physical restraint offers immediate physical control. Any softer techniques of reducing crime cannot count on the same budget. Even if the crime prevention returns are equivalent, many citizens in the United States will be willing to spend much more money to control young men with dark skins than to educate them. This tilt toward punitive programs is exacerbated by the unwillingness of many citizens to fund what appear to be special benefit programs for delinquent and predelinquent youths. Why give the bad ones the cookies? And trying to frighten citizens into support of positive programs will frequently backfire. Extortion never generates good will among its victims.

For all these reasons, diverting resources from punitive to non-punitive modes of crime prevention on a dollar-for-dollar basis is quite unlikely. The political economy of criminal justice and crime prevention in the United States is both more complicated and more discouraging than is comprehended by advocates of youth support through public fear.

The Discouraging Lesson of History

Moreover, the stigma associated with crime prevention undermines the capacity of developmental programs to provide nurture. Efficient crime control singles out children at risk, whereas efficient education and youth development welcome all youths. The problem with calling a program crime prevention is that it *becomes* a program of crime prevention, operating without the optimism and trust that make education work. The negative labels and social stigma of social services motivated by crime worries cannot be neutralized by good intentions or brave words.

The United States is less than a century removed from the most famous episode of nurturance as crime control in human history—the juvenile court. The function of this new court was "not so much to punish as to reform, not to degrade but to uplift, not to crush but to develop, not to make him a criminal but a worthy citizen" (Mack 1909:107). In other words, bring us your delinquents and this new court for children will cure the conditions that cause criminal behavior.

By the 1960s, however, we had learned that negative labels had overpowered the new court's euphemisms and that punitive agendas were commonly pursued. The criminological insights of labeling theory came in no small measure from the twentieth-century history of the juvenile court (Becker 1963; Schur 1973). Many of the juvenile justice reforms of the 1960s and 1970s created programs to divert those who were supposed to be saved by the juvenile court from ever penetrating the court's formal boundaries. Where once the juvenile court was to be a diversion from the punitive and rigid institutions of criminal justice, we have now been at work for decades to divert youths from this first great diversion. And these new diversion programs themselves fall victim to the negative labels and hidden agendas that come from mixing crime prevention motives and social service methods.

The paradox of programs like Head Start, mentoring, adoption, and successful schooling is that nurturant programs work well (and, incidentally, prevent crime) as long as we do not rename and redeploy them as crime control. Social competence comes from empowerment programs open to all children, from programs in which children are expected to succeed. Effects like crime prevention must be incidental to the larger purposes of social programs or they will not be achieved by them.

In one important sense, the self-defeating property of nurturant programs as crime control is good news. Reducing crime is a trivial goal next to the larger interests served by educating and supporting a nation's youths. What Americans can learn from a century of juvenile courts and the rehabilitative ideal is that we must support broad programs of education and training for the right reasons if we are to realize their positive potential. Juvenile courts and offender-based programs can play a modest role in American youth policy, but as soon as social control is the central goal of policy toward the young, this nation will face a problem far more serious than youth crime.

Failures of Perspective

The youth violence scare of the mid-1990s was more a failure of perspective than a misreading of population statistics or crime trends. The arithmetic of population projections was never in dispute—the youth population would grow 16 percent in fifteen years. What allowed observers to make extravagant claims about the size of this increase and its impact was the absence of historical perspective. There was nothing abnormal about the population distribution projected for 2010, but the historical data that make this clear were missing from the discussion.

The arithmetic of crime trends in the late 1980s was also not in dispute. Homicide and assault arrests grew very quickly after the low point reached in the mid-1980s. What allowed observers to assume that rates of offenses would continue to grow, or at least persist at all-time high points, was an absence of historical understanding that violence rates fluctuate in cyclical patterns. The pessimistic straight-line projections had already been ambushed by a down cycle before the ink was dry on their first published versions.

The largest failure of perspective in the youth crime panic of the mid-1990s was a refusal to comprehend the multiple potentials and the contingency of a generation of young children not yet starting school when the bloodbath predictions were made. If the only measure of any generation were the worst acts that any of its members might commit, each new generation in the United States would be viewed as an unqualified disaster. In fact, to see only the negative in any generation of a nation's youths is almost implausibly silly. Such an unbalanced vision of the future can only be put forward by advocates with no real sense of the American past.

This diagnosis leads to one obvious remedial prescription: Each debate about policy toward future cohorts of youth should be grounded on an understanding of the history of youth development as an important part of our national experience. The fearful projections that have of late been shaping attitudes and policy have as their foundation a dangerous innocence that should never be permitted to dominate youth policy again.

References

Allen, Francis. 1996. *The Habits of Legality, Criminal Justice, and the Rule of Law.* New York: Oxford University Press.

Bachman, Jerald, Lloyd Johnston, and Patrick O'Malley. 1984 and 1993. *Monitoring the Future.* Ann Arbor, Mich.: University of Michigan, Institute for Social Research.

Becker, Howard. 1963. *Outsiders: Studies in the Sociology of Deviance.* London: Free Press.

Beckett, Katherine. 1997. *Crime and Drugs in Contemporary American Politics.* New York: Oxford University Press.

Bennett, William, John DiIulio, and John Waters. 1996. *Body Count.* New York: Simon & Schuster.

Bishop, Donna, and Charles Frazier. 1991. "Transfer of Juveniles to Criminal Court: A Case Study and Analysis of Prosecutorial Waiver." *Notre Dame Journal of Law, Ethics and Public Policy* 5:281.

Blackstone, Sir William. 1857. *Commentaries on the Laws of England,* Volume IV. London: Murray.

Blumstein, Alfred. 1995. "Youth Violence, Guns, and the Illicit Drug Industry." *Journal of Criminal Law and Criminology* 86:10.

Blumstein, Alfred, and Richard Rosenfeld. 1998. "Explaining Recent Trends in U.S. Homicide Rates." *Journal of Criminal Law and Criminology.* Forthcoming.

Cook, Philip J. 1991. "The Technology of Personal Violence." In Michael Tonry, ed., *Crime and Justice: An Annual Review of Research.* Chicago: University of Chicago Press.

Cook, Philip J., and John Laub. 1998. "The Unprecedented Epidemic in Youth Violence." In Michael Tonry and Mark Moore, eds., *Youth Violence. Crime and Justice: An Annual Review of Research.* Chicago: University of Chicago Press.

Council on Crime in America. 1996. *The State of Violent Crime in America: A First Report of the Council on Crime in America.* Washington, D.C.: New Citizenship Project.

"The Crime Wave." 1975, June 30. *Time,* p. 10.

Dawson, Robert. 1992. "An Empirical Study of Kent Style Juvenile Transfers to Criminal Court." *St. Mary's Journal* 23:975.

Decker, Scott H. 1996. "Collective and Normative Features of Gang Violence." *Justice Quarterly* 13:243.

DiIulio, John. 1995, November 27. "The Coming of the Super-Predators." *Weekly Standard,* p. 23.

——. 1996. *How to Stop the Coming Crime Wave*. New York: Manhattan Institute.

Dole, Robert. 1996, July 8. Text of Bob Dole Radio Address. *U.S. NewsWire.*

Editorial. 1997, April 28. *Wall Street Journal.*

Eigen, Joel. 1978. The Borderlands of Juvenile Justice: The Waiver Process in Philadelphia. Doctoral dissertation, University of Pennsylvania, Philadelphia.

——. 1981a. "The Determinants and Impact of Jurisdictional Transfer in Philadelphia." In John Hall and Donna Hamparian, eds., *Readings in Public Policy*. Columbus, Ohio: Academy for Contemporary Problems.

——. 1981b. "Punishing Youth Homicide Offenders in Philadelphia." *Journal of Criminal Law and Criminology* 72:3.

Elliott, Delbert. 1994. "Serious Violent Offenders: Onset, Developmental Course, and Termination—The American Society of Criminology 1993 Presidential Address." *Criminology* 32:1.

Elliott, Delbert, and Scott Menard. 1996. "Delinquent Friends and Delinquent Behavior: Temporal and Developmental Patterns." In J. David Hawkins, ed., *Delinquency and Crime: Current Theories*. New York: Cambridge University Press.

Esbensen, Finn-Aage, David Huizinga, and Anne W. Weiher. 1993. "Gang and Non-Gang Youth: Differences in Explanatory Variables." *Journal of Contemporary Criminal Justice* 9:94.

Fagan, Jeffrey A., Martin Forst, and T. Scott Vivona. 1987. "Racial Determinants of the Judicial Transfer Decision: Prosecuting Violent Youth in Criminal Court." *Crime and Delinquency* 33:259.

Farrington, David. 1998. "Predictors, Causes, and Correlates of Youth Violence." In Michael Tonry and Mark Moore, eds., *Crime and Justice: An Annual Review of Research*. Chicago: University of Chicago Press.

Feld, Barry. 1987. "The Juvenile Court Meets the Principle of the Offense." *Journal of Criminal Law and Criminology* 78:471.

——. 1993. "Criminalizing the American Juvenile Court." In Michael Tonry, ed., *Crime and Justice: An Annual Review of Research*. Chicago: The University of Chicago.

——. 1998. "Juvenile and Criminal Justice Systems' Responses to Youth Violence." In Michael Tonry and Mark Moore, eds., *Crime and Justice: An Annual Review of Research*. Chicago: University of Chicago Press.

Fox, James A. 1996. *Trends in Juvenile Violence: A Report to the United States Attorney General on Current and Future Rates of Juvenile Offending*. Boston: Northeastern University Press.

Gardner, Martin. 1997. *Understanding Juvenile Law*. New York: Matthew Bender.

General Accounting Office. 1995. *Juvenile Justice: Juveniles Processed in Criminal Court and Case Dispositions*. Washington, D.C.: U.S. Government Printing Office.

Gest, Ted, and Victoria Pope. 1996, March 25. "Crime Time Bomb." *U.S. News & World Report,* p. 28.

Greenwood, Peter, Karyn E. Model, C. Peter Rydell, and James Chiesa. 1996. *Diverting Children from a Life of Crime.* Santa Monica, Calif.: Rand Corporation.

Greenwood, Peter, Joan Petersilia, and Franklin E. Zimring. 1980. *Age, Crime, and Sanctions: The Transition from Juvenile to Criminal Court.* Santa Monica, Calif.: Rand Corporation.

Greenwood, Peter, and Franklin E. Zimring. 1985. *One More Chance: The Pursuit of Promising Intervention Strategies for Chronic Juvenile Offenders.* Santa Monica, Calif.: Rand Corporation.

Gross, Jane. 1997, July 30. "Experts Testify Shabazz Boy Is Psychotic." *New York Times,* p. B1.

Hawkins, Gordon. 1960. "The Treatment of Violent Criminals." *Criminal Law Review,* p. 689.

Hawkins, Gordon, and Franklin E. Zimring. 1989. *Pornography in a Free Society.* New York: Cambridge University Press.

Hoversten, Paul. 1997, December 2. "In Kentucky, 'Blood Was Everywhere.'" *USA Today,* p. 3.

Howell, James C. 1996, Summer. "The Myth of Related Youth Gang Homicides and Drug Trafficking." *Juvenile and Family Justice Today,* p. 12.

―――. 1998. "Youth Gangs: An Overview." *Office of Juvenile Justice and Delinquency Prevention Research Bulletin.* Washington, D.C.: U.S. Government Printing Office.

Howell, James C., and David Hawkins. 1998. Prevention of Youth Violence. In Michael Tonry and Mark Moore, eds., *Crime and Justice: An Annual Review of Research.* Chicago: University of Chicago Press.

Hutzler, John. 1982. "Cannon to the Left, Canon to the Right: Can the Juvenile Court Survive?" *Today's Delinquent* 1:25.

Institute for Judicial Administration. 1977. *Standards for Juvenile Justice,* Vols. 1–2. New York: Institute for Judicial Administration.

Kadish, Sanford. 1985. "Complicity, Cause, and Blame." *California Law Review* 73:323.

Lacayo, Richard. 1994, September 19. "When Kids Go Bad." *Time,* p. 60.

Lott, John, and David Mustard. 1997. "Crime, Deterrence and Right-to-Carry Concealed Handguns." *The Journal of Legal Studies* 26:1.

Lyons, Donna. 1997, May. "Juvenile Justice Comes of Age." *State Legislatures,* p. 12.

Mack, Julian W. 1909. "The Juvenile Court." *Harvard Law Review* 23:104.

McCollum, Bill. 1996, April 30. Testimony Before the House Subcommittee on Early Childhood, Youth, and Families. Washington, D.C.: U.S. Government Printing Office.

McNulty, Paul J. 1995. "Natural Born Killers? Preventing the Coming Explosion of Teenage Crime." *Policy Review* 71:84.

Merton, Robert K. 1967. *Social Theory and Social Structure.* New York: Macmillan.

Moffitt, Terrie. 1993. "Adolescent-Limited and Life Courses Persistant Behavior: A Developmental Taxonomy." *Psychological Bulletin,* p. 100.

Morris, Norval. 1977. "Punishment, Desert, and Rehabilitation." Bicentennial Lecture, U.S. Department of Justice, Washington, D.C.

National Center for Health Statistics. 1991. *Vital Statistics of the United States.* Washington, D.C.: U.S. Government Printing Office.

Newton, George, and Franklin E. Zimring. 1969. *Firearms and Violence in American Life,* Task Force Report to the National Commission on the Causes and Prevention of Violence. Washington, D.C.: U.S. Government Printing Office.

Patterson, Orlando. 1997, November 16. "Racism Is Not the Issue." *New York Times,* p. A15.

Peltier, Michael. 1997, August 29. "Florida Teen Guilty in British Tourist Shooting." *Reuters.*

Podger, Pamela. 1995, October 18. "Latest Reynolds Effort Will Target Gun Crimes." *Fresno Bee,* p. A1.

Redding, Richard E. 1997. "Juveniles Transferred to Criminal Court: Legal Reform Proposals Based on Social Science Research." *Utah Law Review* 1997:709.

Reiss, Albert. 1986. "Co-offending Influences on Criminal Careers." In Alfred Blumstein, Jacqueline Cohen, Jeffrey Roth, and Christy Visher, eds., *Criminal Careers and "Career Criminals,"* Vol. 2. Washington D.C.: National Academy Press.

Rothman, David. 1980. *Conscience and Convenience: The Asylum and Its Alternatives in Progressive America.* Boston: Little, Brown.

Schemo, Diana Jean. 1997, December 6. "In Venezuela, 'Year of Rights,' the Police Kill More Youths." *New York Times,* p. A1.

Schneider, Anne L., and Donna Schram. 1983. *A Justice Philosophy for the Juvenile Court.* Seattle, Wash.: Urban Policy Research.

Schur, Edwin. 1973. *Radical Nonintervention: Rethinking the Delinquency Problem.* Englewood Cliffs, N.J.: Prentice Hall.

Schwartz, Stephen. 1997, June 28. "Accused Killer Will Be Tried as an Adult." *San Francisco Chronicle,* p. A17.

Senate Committee on the Judiciary. 1996, March 12. Senator Fred Thompson, Remarks of the Chair Introducing Hearings of the Subcommittee on Youth Violence, RG 46, National Archives, Washington, D.C.

Shannon, Lyle, Judith L. McKim, Kathleen R. Anderson, and William E. Murph. 1991. *Changing Patterns of Delinquency and Crime: A Longitudinal Study in Racine.* Boulder, Colo.: Westview Press.

Silberman, Charles. 1978. *Criminal Violence, Criminal Justice.* New York: Random House.

Singer, Simon. 1996. *Recriminalizing Delinquency: Violent Juvenile Crime and Juvenile Justice Reform.* New York: Cambridge University Press.

Snyder, Howard N. 1998. "Serious, Violent and Chronic Juvenile Offenders: An Assessment of the Extent of and Trends in Officially-Recognized Serious Criminal Behavior in a Delinquent Population." In Rolf Loeber and David Farrington, eds., *Never Too Early, Never Too Late: Risk Factors and Successful Interventions for Serious and Violent Juvenile Offenders.* Thousand Oaks, Calif.: Sage.

Snyder, Howard, and Melissa Sickmund. 1995. *Juvenile Offenders and*

Victims: A National Report. Washington, D.C.: U.S. Government Printing Office.

Steinberg, Laurence, and Elizabeth Cauffman. 1996. "Maturity of Judgment in Adolescence: Psychosocial Factors in Adolescent Decision-making Law and Human Behavior." *Law and Human Behavior* 29:249.

Texas Juvenile Probation Commission. 1984–1986, 1994–1996. *Texas Juvenile Probation Statistical Report.* Austin: Texas Juvenile Probation Commission.

Torbet, Patricia, Richard Gable, Hunter Hurst IV, Imogene Montgomery, Linda Szymanski, and Douglas Thomas. 1996. *State Responses to Serious and Violent Juvenile Crime.* Washington, D.C.: U.S. Government Printing Office.

Twentieth Century Fund. 1978. *Confronting Youth Crime.* New York: Holmes & Meier.

United Kingdom Office of National Statistics. 1997. *Social Trends 27.* London: Her Majesty's Stationery Office.

"Upsurge in Violent Crime by Youngsters." 1978, July 17. *U.S. News & World Report,* p. 55.

U.S. Department of Commerce, Bureau of the Census. 1960–1994, 1995a. *Current Population Reports: Estimates of the Population of the United States by Age, Sex, and Race.* Washington, D.C.: U.S. Government Printing Office.

———. 1995b. *Statistical Abstract of the United States.* Washington D.C.: U.S. Government Printing Office.

U.S. Department of Justice, Bureau of Justice Statistics. 1980–1992. *Criminal Victimization in the United States.* Washington, DC: U.S. Government Printing Office.

U.S. Department of Justice, Federal Bureau of Investigation. 1976–1993, 1994a, 1995–1996. *Crime in the United States.* Washington, D.C.: U.S. Government Printing Office.

———. 1994b. *Uniform Crime Reports: Supplementary Homicide Reports, 1976–1992.* 1st ICPSR version.

Vila, Bryan. 1997. "Human Nature and Crime Control: Improving the Feasibility of Nurturant Strategies." *Politics and the Life Sciences* 16:1.

Virginia Governor's Commission on Juvenile Justice. 1995. *Final Report.* Richmond, Va.: Department of Criminal Justice Services.

Vorenberg, James, and Elizabeth Vorenberg. 1973. "Early Diversion From the Criminal Justice System: A Practice in Search of a Theory." In Lloyd Ohlin, ed., *Prisoners in America.* Englewood Cliffs, N.J.: Prentice Hall.

Walker, Thaai, and Elaine Herscher. 1997, March 12. "Oakland Girl Shot by Schoolmate." *San Francisco Chronicle,* p. A17.

Warr, Mark. 1996. "Organization and Instigation in Delinquent Groups." *Criminology* 34:11.

Wilson, James Q. 1974. *Thinking About Crime.* New York: Basic Books.

———. 1995. "Crime and Public Policy." In James Q. Wilson and Joan

Petersilia, eds., *Crime*. San Francisco: Institute for Contemporary Studies Press.

Wilson, James Q., and Joan Petersilia, eds. 1995. *Crime*. San Francisco: Institute for Contemporary Studies Press.

Wilson, Pete. 1997, August 25. Letter to the California Senate (Returning Senate Bill 669 Without Signature).

Wolfgang, Marvin, Robert Figlio, and Thorsten Sellin. 1972. *Delinquency in a Birth Cohort*. Chicago: University of Chicago Press.

Zimring, Franklin E. 1968. "Is Gun Control Likely to Reduce Violent Killings?" *University of Chicago Law Review* 35:721.

———. 1972. "The Medium is the Message: Firearms Caliber as a Determinant of the Death Rate from Assault." *Journal of Legal Studies* 1:97.

———. 1975. "Firearms and Federal Law: The Gun Control Act of 1968." *Journal of Legal Studies* 4:133.

———. 1978. *Confronting Youth Crime: Report of the Twentieth Century Fund Task Force on Sentencing Policy Toward Young Offenders*. New York: Holmes & Meier.

———. 1979. "American Youth Violence: Issues and Trends." In Norval Morris and Michael Tonry, eds., *Crime and Justice: An Annual Review of Research*. Chicago: University of Chicago Press.

———. 1981. "Kids, Groups, and Crime: Some Implications of a Well-known Secret." *Journal of Criminal Law and Criminology* 72:867.

———. 1982. *The Changing Legal World of Adolescence*. New York: Free Press.

———. 1991. "The Treatment of Hard Cases in American Juvenile Justice: In Defense of Discretionary Waiver." *Notre Dame Journal of Law, Ethics, and Public Policy* 5:267.

———. 1996. "Kids, Guns, and Homicide: Policy Notes on an Age-specific Epidemic." *Law and Contemporary Problems* 59:25.

Zimring, Franklin E., Joel Eigen, and Sheila O'Malley. 1976. "Punishing Homicide in Philadelphia: Perspectives on the Death Penalty." *University of Chicago Law Review* 43:227.

Zimring, Franklin E., and Gordon Hawkins. 1987. *The Cititzen's Guide to Gun Control*. New York: Macmillan.

———. 1992. *Prison Population and Criminal Justice Policy in California*. Berkeley, Calif.: Institute of Governmental Studies.

———. 1997. *Crime Is Not the Problem: Lethal Violence in America*. New York: Oxford University Press.

———. 1997. "Generations at Risk? Generational Influences on Youth Development." Working Paper No. 26. Berkeley, Calif.: Earl Warren Legal Institute.

———. 1998. "Toward a Jurisprudence of Youth Violence." In Michael Tonry and Mark Moore, eds., *Crime and Justice: An Annual Review of Research*. Chicago: University of Chicago Press.

Zimring, Franklin E., and James Zuehl. 1986. "Victim Injury and Death in Urban Robbery: A Chicago Study." *The Journal of Legal Studies* 15:1.

Index